Regulating Vessel Discharges on the International and EU Level

# The Law of the Sea



Volumes published in this Brill Research Perspectives title are listed at *brill.com/rpls*

# Regulating Vessel Discharges on the International and EU Level

*The Examples of Scrubber Washwater, Sewage and Ballast Water*

*By*

Alexander Proelss
Valentin J. Schatz

BRILL

LEIDEN | BOSTON

This paperback book edition is simultaneously published as issue 3.3–4 of *Law of the Sea*, DOI:10.1163/24519359-12340009.

Library of Congress Control Number: 2021939633

Typeface for the Latin, Greek, and Cyrillic scripts: "Brill". See and download: brill.com/brill-typeface.

ISBN 978-90-04-47032-3 (paperback)
ISBN 978-90-04-47033-0 (e-book)



This book is printed on acid-free paper and produced in a sustainable manner.

# Contents

# Regulating Vessel Discharges on the International and EU Level

***The Examples of Scrubber Washwater, Sewage and Ballast Water***

*Alexander Proelss*
Professor of Law, Chair in the International Law of the Sea and International Environmental Law, Public International Law and Public Law, Institute for the Law of the Sea and Maritime Law, Faculty of Law, University of Hamburg
*alexander.proelss@uni-hamburg.de*

*Valentin J. Schatz*
Research Associate, Institute for the Law of the Sea and Maritime Law, Faculty of Law, University of Hamburg
*valentin.schatz@uni-hamburg.de*

## Abstract

This study analyzes the legal requirements concerning discharges from ships, a matter that is characterized by a considerable degree of complexity. This complexity results, *inter alia*, from the highly technical nature of the applicable norms, but also from the fact that the relevant rules and principles are prescribed in a wide and often overlapping variety of instruments on different levels of law, namely public international law, European Union law (where applicable) and domestic law. Taking into account that the individual legal instruments within these sub-systems of law significantly differ in their spatial and substantive scopes and regulatory approaches, a risk of conflicts of norms exists both from a vertical (i.e., between different levels of law) and horizontal (i.e., between different instruments on the same level of law) perspective. This situation gives rise to legal uncertainties, which may ultimately threaten the lawful and effective application and implementation of the relevant norms. This study attempts to clarify the existing uncertainties and to suggest harmonized interpretations and applications of the pertinent rules and principles. It does not address the issue of pollution from ships in general, but focuses on three specific categories of vessel discharges, namely scrubber washwater, sewage and ballast water.

 | DOI:10.1163/9789004470330_002

**Keywords**

marine pollution – vessel discharges – sulphur emissions – scrubber washwater – ballast water – sewage

## 1 Introduction

Although shipping is generally considered to be a relatively environmentally friendly category of transport when compared to land and aerial transport, it has always been one of the main sources of marine pollution. The operation of ships can create various forms of pollution, which include oil pollution, chemical pollution, discharges of sewage and garbage, and air pollution caused by emissions (including SOx, NOx and particulate matter). In addition, the operation of ships can spread alien invasive aquatic species and thereby present a threat to marine ecosystems. The international community sought to take account of this fact at an early stage by adopting a host of multilateral treaties dealing with this source of pollution, particularly under the auspices of the International Maritime Organization (IMO).[1] Among the first of these treaties was the 1954 International Convention for the Prevention of Pollution of the Sea by Oil (OILPOL),[2] which was later replaced by the 1973 International Convention for the Prevention of Pollution from Ships (MARPOL Convention)[3] and its Annexes.[4] Today, Part XII of the 1982 United Nations Convention on the Law of the Sea (UNCLOS)[5] establishes the general international legal framework for the protection and preservation of the marine environment, which is then further developed by the agreements and measures adopted within the

1 IMO, 'List of IMO Conventions' 2020, at: <http://www.imo.org/en/About/Conventions/ListOfConventions/Pages/Default.aspx> (accessed 17 November 2020).

2 *International Convention for the Prevention of Pollution of the Sea by Oil*, adopted 12 May 1954, entered into force 26 July 1958, 327 UNTS 3.

3 *International Convention for the Prevention of Pollution from Ships*, adopted 2 November 1973, entered into force 2 October 1983, 1340 UNTS 184. See also *Protocol of 1978 relating to the International Convention for the Prevention of Pollution from Ships, 1973*, adopted 17 February 1978, entered into force 2 October 1983, 1340 UNTS 61.

4 For an overview, see IMO, 'International Convention for the Prevention of Pollution from Ships (MARPOL)' 2020, at: <https://www.imo.org/en/About/Conventions/Pages/International-Convention-for-the-Prevention-of-Pollution-from-Ships-(MARPOL).aspx> (accessed 17 November 2020).

5 *United Nations Convention on the Law of the Sea*, adopted 10 December 1982, entered into force 16 November 1994, 1833 UNTS 3.

IMO specifically dedicated to the prevention and regulation of marine pollution from ships, in particular the MARPOL Convention and its Annexes.[6]

Some of the aforementioned forms of pollution or introduction of alien invasive species result from vessel discharges into the sea. This study examines the legal measures by which the international community has addressed discharges from ships on a global and regional level. For the purposes of this analysis, the regulatory activity and practice of the European Union (EU) serves as a regional case-study. The EU was chosen for these purposes because (1) it represents a large and relatively unitary block of States that includes several important maritime States, (2) it has a shared regulatory competence for marine environmental issues and shipping, and (3) it frequently acts as an innovator in the regulation of shipping – sometimes by way of unilateral regulation which may contradict, or is sometimes even implemented with the aim to strengthen, the relevant global rules and standards.[7]

In view of their practical relevance and the fact that legal scholarship has so far paid only marginal attention to the (often technical) details of the international and European regulation of vessel discharges,[8] this study focuses on three distinct but at the same time closely related categories of vessel discharges, namely, (1) washwater from exhaust gas cleaning systems ("scrubbers"), (2) sewage, and (3) ballast water. While the former two categories

6 On today's international marine environmental law, see generally J. Harrison, *Saving the Oceans Through Law: The International Legal Framework for the Protection of the Marine Environment* (Oxford University Press: Oxford, 2017).

7 See, e.g., V. Frank, *The European Community and Marine Environmental Protection in the International Law of the Sea: Implementing Global Obligations at the Regional Level* (Martinus Nijhoff Publishers: Leiden, 2007); H. Ringbom, *The EU Maritime Safety Policy and International Law* (Martinus Nijhoff Publishers: Leiden, 2008); I. Christodoulou-Varotsi: *Maritime Safety Law and Policies of the European Union and the United States of America: Antagonism or Synergy?* (Springer: Berlin, 2009); M. Höltmann, *Schiffssicherheit und Meeresumweltschutz in der EU nach Erika und Prestige: Die Vereinbarkeit der Gesetzesmaßnahmen der EU mit dem internationalen Seerecht* (Nomos: Baden-Baden, 2012); A. Stöfen-O'Brien, *The International and European Legal Regime Regulating Marine Litter in the EU* (Nomos: Baden-Baden, 2015); M. Gilek and K. Kern (eds.), *Governing Europe's Marine Environment: Europeanization of Regional Seas or Regionalisation of EU Policies?* (Routledge: Abingdon, 2015); K. Solf, *Europäisches Meeresumweltrecht im Internationalen Mehrebenensystem: Grenzen und Möglichkeiten eines europäischen Meeresumweltrechts am Beispiel europäischer und internationaler Vorgaben zur Eindämmung von Schiffsemissionen* (Nomos: Baden-Baden, 2017); N. F. Coelho, *Unilateral Port State Jurisdiction: The Quest for Universality in the Prevention, Reduction and Control of Ship-source Pollution* (Utrecht University: Utrecht, 2019), <https://www.uu.nl/sites/default/files/rebo-nelson-coelho-54375_thesis-ilovepdf-compressed.pdf> (accessed 7 March 2021).

8 As far as can be seen, there is a lack of relevant legal assessments especially in the field of English language scholarship.

of discharges are, as far as international law is concerned, primarily addressed by the MARPOL Convention and its Annexes, the latter is regulated by a specific treaty, the 2004 International Convention for the Control and Management of Ships' Ballast Water and Sediments (BWM Convention),[9] which entered into force on 8 September 2017.[10] In addition to these treaties, vessel discharges are governed by various other international and, within Europe, EU legal instruments.

What is common to the MARPOL Convention, the BWM Convention, and the many other applicable international instruments governing pollution from ships is that their aim is to prevent pollution of the marine environment by discharges that are created by the *operation* of ships. In contrast, pollution by intentional dumping of waste or harmful substances is governed by a distinct regime, namely the rules and principles codified in the 1972 London Convention and its 1996 Protocol.[11] Neither such intentional forms of pollution nor pollution of the marine environment arising from ship accidents are included in the scope of this study.

Overall, the legal regime governing discharges from ships is characterized by an overlap and interaction of different legal frameworks operating at different levels (international law of the sea, international environmental law, EU law, domestic law). It is also characterized by selectivity, a high degree of technicality, and, in particular, its fragmentary character. Particularly in view of the need to effectively apply and implement the relevant rules and standards in legal practice, the aforementioned features result, to a certain extent, in legal uncertainty and ambiguity, which the present study is intended to address.

Against this background, this study comprehensively examines the relevant provisions of international and EU law, with specific reference to the abovementioned discharge categories. It first analyzes the legal regime governing the operation of exhaust gas cleaning systems, and the washwater discharges that may result from these systems. Second, it focuses on the legal requirements that apply to sewage discharges. Third, it examines the legal rules and principles addressing ballast water discharges. In doing so, it aims to identify

9 *International Convention for the Control and Management of Ships' Ballast Water and Sediments*, adopted 13 February 2004, entered into force 8 September 2017, UNTS Registration No. 55544.

10 See generally IMO, 'Ballast Water Management' 2020, at: <https://www.imo.org/en/OurWork/Environment/Pages/BallastWaterManagement.aspx> (accessed 17 November 2020).

11 *Convention on the Prevention of Marine Pollution by Dumping of Wastes and Other Matter*, adopted 29 December 1972, entered into force 30 August 1975, 1046 UNTS 120; *Protocol to the Convention on the Prevention of Marine Pollution by Dumping of Wastes and Other Matter, 1972*, adopted 7 November 1996, entered into force 24 March 2006, (1997) 36 ILM 1.

parallels and differences as well as gaps in the current legal regime of vessel discharges in order to contribute to the further development of the field concerned. Throughout the study, special attention is paid to the geographical and substantive scope of the relevant legal instruments, and to the prevention and resolution of potential overlaps and conflicts between the relevant instruments.

## 2 Discharges of Washwater from Exhaust Gas Cleaning Systems

In order to comply with international emission standards,[12] exhaust gas cleaning systems ("scrubbers") are increasingly used in the operation of seagoing vessels. These systems are designed to remove pollutants from exhaust gas of ships,[13] thereby complementing the gradual transition towards more environment-friendly ship fuels that avoid problematic concentrations of pollutants in exhaust from the outset.[14] A distinction must be made between dry and wet scrubbers.[15] Dry scrubbers, which have remained relatively low in number compared to wet scrubbers, clean exhaust gases with hydrated lime-treated granulates rather than liquids, resulting in no discharges into the sea.[16] Wet scrubbers, which are the focus of the present study, bring the exhaust gases from ship engines into contact with a liquid (usually seawater or freshwater as well as caustic soda). Pollutants such as sulphur oxides (SOx) and nitrogen oxides (NOx), which are formed during the combustion of ship fuel, are thereby washed out of the exhaust gas. The washwater produced in this process can be contaminated, e.g., with heavy metals, and often has a very low pH value. Different types of wet scrubber systems exist. "Open loop" scrubbers use seawater, which is partially discharged into the sea after the cleaning process. Filtered particles or residues (so-called scrubber sludge) are usually collected in a separate tank and can be disposed of separately. In contrast,

12 IMO, 'Sulphur oxides (SOx) and Particulate Matter (PM) – Regulation 14' 2020, at: <https://www.imo.org/en/OurWork/Environment/Pages/Sulphur-oxides-(SOx)-%E2%80%93-Regulation-14.aspx> (accessed 17 November 2020); IMO, 'Sulphur 2020: Cutting Sulphur Oxide Emissions' 2020, at: <https://www.imo.org/en/MediaCentre/HotTopics/Pages/Sulphur-2020.aspx> (accessed 17 November 2020).

13 See generally E. den Boer and M. Hoen, *Scrubbers: An Economic and Ecological Assessment* (CE Delft: Delft, 2015).

14 IMO, 'Equivalents (SOx scrubber, etc.) – Regulation 4' 2020, at: <https://www.imo.org/en/OurWork/Environment/Pages/Equivalents-(Sox-scrubber,-etc.)---Regulation-4.aspx> (accessed 17 November 2020).

15 Cf. Boer and Hoen (n. 13), at 11.

16 Ibid.

"closed loop" scrubbers usually use freshwater, which circulates in the scrubber system until it is fully loaded. In this process, the scrubber sludge is also filtered out and collected separately. Some closed loop scrubbers, however, discharge a small portion of the scrubber sludge into the water. There are also "hybrid" scrubbers, which can switch between open loop and closed loop operation as required. Therefore, the use of scrubbers – particularly open loop and hybrid models – can involve scrubber washwater being discharged into the sea, which in turn can result in pollution of the environment.[17] Environmental risks are particularly noteworthy in areas where there is a high concentration of scrubber washwater discharges, such as seaports and estuaries.[18]

## 2.1 *International Regulation of Scrubber Washwater Discharges*

### 2.1.1 Prohibition of Transfer and Transformation of Pollution

As the central framework agreement in the international law of the sea, UNCLOS contains fundamental provisions on marine environmental protection in its Part XII (Articles 192–237). These provisions are primarily, though not exclusively,[19] aimed at regulating marine pollution.[20] According to Article 192 of UNCLOS, "States have the obligation to protect and preserve the marine environment". It is now recognized that the scope of this fundamental obligation – as well as other general provisions of Part XII – is geographically unlimited as far as the marine environment is concerned and, therefore, applies to all maritime zones.[21]

---

17 See generally J. Kjølholt, S. Aakre, C. Jürgensen et al., *Assessment of Possible Impacts of Scrubber Water Discharges on the Marine Environment* (Miljøstyrelsen: Copenhagen, 2012).

18 See, e.g., J. Teuchies, T. J. S. Cox, K. van Itterbeeck et al. 'The Impact of Scrubber Discharge on the Water Quality in Estuaries and Ports' (2020) 32 *Environmental Sciences Europe* <https://doi.org/10.1186/s12302-020-00380-z> (accessed 17 November 2020); J. Faber, B. van Hattum and F. Kleissen, *The Impacts of EGCS Washwater Discharges on Port Water and Sediment* (CE Delft: Delft, 2019).

19 *Chagos Marine Protected Area Arbitration* (*Mauritius v. United Kingdom*), Award, 18 March 2015, PCA Case No. 2011-03, [320]. See also *South China Sea Arbitration* (*Republic of the Philippines v. People's Republic of China*), Award, 12 July 2016, PCA Case No. 2013-19, [945].

20 D. Czybulka, 'Article 192', in A. Proelss (ed), *United Nations Convention on the Law of the Sea (UNCLOS): A Commentary* (C. H. Beck/Hart/Nomos: Munich/Oxford/Baden-Baden, 2017), 1277, at [3].

21 See, e.g., *Request for an Advisory Opinion Submitted by the Sub-Regional Fisheries Commission (SRFC)*, Advisory Opinion, 2 April 2015, *ITLOS Reports* 2015, 4, [120]; *Dispute Concerning Coastal State Rights in the Black Sea, Sea of Azov, and Kerch Strait* (*Ukraine v. the Russian Federation*), Award concerning the Preliminary Objections of the Russian Federation, 21 February 2020, PCA Case No. 2017-06, [295].

Article 192 of UNCLOS is further developed by Articles 194–196. Article 194(1) of UNCLOS contains an obligation to take all measures necessary to prevent, reduce and control pollution of the marine environment from any source. Article 194(2) of UNCLOS further requires States Parties to take all necessary measures "to ensure that activities under their jurisdiction or control are so conducted as not to cause damage by pollution to other States and their environment". Article 211(1) of UNCLOS specifies the way in which these obligations shall be implemented in relation to pollution from ships: "States, acting through the competent international organization or general diplomatic conference, shall establish international rules and standards to prevent, reduce and control pollution of the marine environment from vessels". The "competent international organization" in terms of this provision is the IMO.[22] Article 211(2) of UNCLOS also obliges States Parties to adopt laws and regulations to this end in their domestic law and prescribes that these measures must "at least have the same effect as that of generally accepted international rules and standards".

The use of exhaust gas cleaning systems serves the purpose of fulfilling these obligations with regard to the reduction of SOx emissions that cause damage to, *inter alia*, the marine environment.[23] However, the fact that such systems cause a partial transformation of one form of pollution – the emission of SOx into the atmosphere – into another form – discharges of harmful washwater into the marine environment – casts doubts as to whether their operation is compatible with Article 195 of UNCLOS.[24] This provision states that "[i]n taking measures to prevent, reduce and control pollution of the marine environment, States shall act so as not to transfer, directly or indirectly, damage or hazards from one area to another or transform one type of pollution into another".

Similar to Articles 192 and 194 of UNCLOS, Article 195 is applicable in all maritime zones.[25] Its purpose is to prevent any circumvention by the parties to the Convention of the various obligations codified in Part XII of UNCLOS (in particular those prescribed by Article 194(1) and (2)) by transferring damage or hazards or by transforming one form of pollution into another.[26] Article 195

22 K. Bartenstein, 'Article 211', in Proelss (ed.) (n. 20), 1419, at [14].

23 T. Markus and L. P. Helfst, 'Regulierung der Einleitung von Abwasser aus Schiffsabgasreinigungsanlagen zum Schutz der Meere' (2014) 36 *Natur und Recht* 760, at 762.

24 A. Proelß and V. J. Schatz, *Rechtliche Vorgaben zum Umgang mit Schiffsabwasser: Völker-, unions- und nationalrechtliche Anforderungen an Einleitungen von Scrubber-Abwasser, Ballastwasser und häuslichem Abwasser durch Schiffe* (Umweltbundesamt: Dessau-Roßlau, 2019), at 39.

25 Czybulka (n. 20), at [15].

26 Proelß and Schatz (n. 24), at 39.

of UNCLOS must thus be read in conjunction with Article 194,[27] and it also applies to measures taken by international organizations or agreements and measures adopted within the framework of international organizations, such as the MARPOL Convention and its Annexes.[28]

When assessing whether the operation of exhaust gas cleaning systems is compatible with the prohibition of transformation of pollution, it is important to note that Article 195 of UNCLOS not only covers the direct or indirect transformation of one type of water pollution into another, but also the transformation of ship emissions into discharges from vessels.[29] As Article 195 of UNCLOS thus requires – in principle – that the necessary measures be taken at source and that the costs thereof be borne by the polluter,[30] the prohibition of transformation is conceptionally linked to the polluter pays and origin principles.[31] Indeed, Article 195 of UNCLOS is based on a holistic approach to marine environmental protection by including all sources of pollution.[32]

UNCLOS defines "pollution of the marine environment" as "the introduction by man, directly or indirectly, of substances or energy into the marine environment, including estuaries, which results or is likely to result in such deleterious effects as harm to living resources and marine life, hazards to human health, hindrance to marine activities, including fishing and other legitimate uses of the sea, impairment of quality for use of sea water and reduction of amenities".[33] Taking into account the risk of contamination involved in the operation of open scrubber systems, there is no doubt that the discharge of scrubber washwater must be classified as "pollution of the marine environment".[34] Furthermore, the discharge of scrubber washwater also constitutes a "transformation" within the meaning of Article 195 of UNCLOS:[35] while vessel-based emissions of pollutants into the atmosphere decrease, the quantity of pollutants that are introduced into the marine environment increases.

It should be noted, though, that Article 195 of UNCLOS does arguably not establish an absolute prohibition which renders any kind of transformation of

27 Czybulka (n. 20), at [15].
28 Ibid., at [11].
29 Ibid., at [3].
30 See also ibid., at [4].
31 A. Proelß, *Meeresschutz im Völker- und Europarecht: Das Beispiel des Nordostatlantiks* (Duncker & Humblot: Berlin, 2004), at 84; Markus and Helfst (n. 23), at 761.
32 Ibid.
33 UNCLOS, Art. 1(1)(4).
34 B. Lange, T. Markus and Lutz P. Helfst, *Impacts of Scrubbers on the Environmental Situation in Ports and Coastal Waters* (Umweltbundesamt: Dessau-Roßlau, 2014), 52–53. See also Markus and Helfst (n. 23), at 762; Proelß and Schatz (n. 24), at 40.
35 Cf. Lange, Markus and Helfst (n. 34), at 53.

pollution unlawful.[36] Indeed, absolute prohibitions are foreign to Part XII of UNCLOS and would in some cases even be contrary to its objectives. It cannot be excluded, for example, that in certain situations transformations of pollution may constitute a significant reduction of emissions in one medium, and the resulting pollution of another medium may be less significant or even insignificant.[37] If disproportionate costs were to be incurred for the complete avoidance of transformations that would cause only insignificant damage to another environmental medium, this would arguably be contrary to the principle of proportionality.[38] Therefore, Article 195 of UNCLOS should be held to merely embody a prohibition *in principle*, which, in the case of a planned transformation, requires a balancing exercise in the sense of a proportionality test.[39] As discussed below, this interpretation of Article 195 of UNCLOS is confirmed by the existing practice of the IMO under the MARPOL Convention, especially with regard to washwater from exhaust gas cleaning systems. Due to the IMO's role as competent international organization within the meaning of Article 211(1) of UNCLOS, its practice is of particular importance in this respect.[40]

Article 195 of UNCLOS is directed to all States Parties, which are thus called upon to implement the prohibition of transformation in their domestic legislation as well as regional regulatory fora. In this respect, they are under a duty to protect and preserve the marine environment, but, as can also be demonstrated by reference to Article 193 of UNCLOS, are not subject to an *absolute* prohibition of *any* kind of pollution. Thus, while the discharge of scrubber washwater cannot be held to be completely prohibited by Article 195 of UNCLOS,[41] States must carefully examine in each case whether the advantages of using such technologies outweigh the disadvantages and risks for the marine environment, and whether it is not perhaps necessary to prohibit such discharges entirely.[42] When conducting this balancing exercise, the relevant provisions of the specifically applicable international treaties, in particular those of the MARPOL Convention, must be taken into account. The general obligation of the States Parties regarding the protection of the marine environment also militates in favour of limiting in time the use of technologies by which one type of pollution is transformed into another, not entirely insignificant type

36 Proelß and Schatz (n. 24), at 40.
37 Ibid., at 41.
38 Ibid.
39 Ibid.
40 Ibid.
41 Ibid. Contra: Lange, Markus and Helfst (n. 34), at 54; Markus and Helfst (n. 23), at 762.
42 Proelß and Schatz (n. 24), at 41.

of marine pollution.[43] In the light of the precautionary principle, which must implicitly be read into Part XII of UNCLOS,[44] this should apply in particular where there is scientific uncertainty as to the extent of the adverse effects of the technology.

### 2.1.2 Annex VI to the MARPOL Convention

#### 2.1.2.1 *Objectives and Scope*

The MARPOL Convention is a framework convention negotiated within the IMO and has been in force since 1 January 1983. Its significance can only be grasped by reference to its six Annexes, each of which is devoted to a ship-related type of pollution: oil (Annex I); noxious liquid substances in bulk (Annex II); harmful substances carried by sea in packaged form (Annex III); sewage from ships (Annex IV); garbage from ships (Annex V); and air pollution from ships (Annex VI).[45] As shown by this brief enumeration, the object and purpose of the MARPOL Convention is to prevent pollution of the sea by "operational" discharges that are created by the operation of ships.

Neither the MARPOL Convention itself nor its Annexes or other relevant IMO documents clearly define the spatial scope of the MARPOL Convention. Article 3 of the MARPOL Convention merely states to which ships the MARPOL Convention applies. However, the definition of the term "ship" in Article 2(4) of the MARPOL Convention refers to "ships of any type *operating in the marine environment*".[46] This definition, when considered in conjunction with the MARPOL Convention's objectives,[47] militates in favour of accepting that the internal waters (which are, as can be demonstrated by reference to Article 218 of UNCLOS, also included in the scope of Part XII of UNCLOS) are covered by the

---

43 Ibid.

44 *Southern Bluefin Tuna Cases* (*New Zealand v. Japan; Australia v. Japan*), Provisional Measures, Order of 27 August 1999, *ITLOS Reports* 1999, 280, [77]; S. Marr, *The Precautionary Principle in the Law of the Sea: Modern Decision Making in International Law* (Martinus Nijhoff: Leiden, 2003), at 52; D. Freestone, 'International Fisheries Law since Rio: The Continued Rise of the Precautionary Principle', in: A. E. Boyle and D. Freestone (eds), *International Law and Sustainable Development: Past Achievements and Future Challenges* (Oxford University Press: Oxford, 1999), 135–164, at 138; B. Sage-Fuller, *The Precautionary Principle in Marine Environmental Law: With Special Reference to High Risk Vessels* (Routledge: London, 2015), at 68; D. Czybulka, 'Article 196', in Proelss (ed) (n. 20), at 1319, [9, 19]; T. Stephens, 'Article 198', in Proelss (ed) (n. 20), 1333, at [13]; Proelß and Schatz (n. 24), at 41.

45 For an overview, see IMO (n. 4).

46 Italics added. See MARPOL Convention, Art. 1(4): "vessel of any type whatsoever operating in the marine environment and includes hydrofoil boats, air-cushion vehicles, submersibles, floating craft and fixed or floating platforms".

47 Cf. MARPOL Convention, Art. 1.

scope of the MARPOL Convention.[48] Article 4(2) of the MARPOL Convention, which provides that "any violation of the requirements of the [MARPOL Convention] within the jurisdiction of any Party to the [MARPOL] Convention shall be prohibited and sanctions shall be established therefor under the law of that Party" equally presupposes the inclusion of internal waters into the MARPOL regime.[49] In addition, Article 5(2) of the MARPOL Convention prescribes an obligation of a ship to carry certificates and to tolerate inspections while *in the ports or offshore terminals* under the jurisdiction of a Contracting Party. Finally, Article 3(1)(a) of Directive (EC) 2005/35 on Ship-source Pollution and on the Introduction of Penalties for Infringements[50] states that the Directive applies "in accordance with international law, to discharges of polluting substances in […] the internal waters, including ports, of a Member State, in so far as the [MARPOL] regime is applicable", a fact that further suggests that the MARPOL Convention is regarded as generally applying in the internal waters, including seaports of its States Parties, subject to the existence of special arrangements in its Annexes.[51]

#### 2.1.2.2 *Substantive Provisions concerning Scrubber Washwater Discharges*

While discharges of sewage from ships are regulated in Annex IV to the MARPOL Convention and pollution caused by discharges of oil in Annex I to the MARPOL Convention, scrubber washwater is peculiar because it is generated

48 Proelß and Schatz, (n. 24), at 41–42; *Request for an Advisory Opinion Submitted by the Sub-Regional Fisheries Commission (SRFC)* (n. 21), at [120]. Note that the inclusion of the internal waters into the UNCLOS regime has recently become contentious following the decision of the ITLOS in *The "ARA Libertad" Case (Argentina v. Ghana)*, Provisional Measures, Order of 15 December 2012, *ITLOS Reports* 2012, 332. Ultimately, the Tribunal took no position on this question beyond the applicability of individual provisions of UNCLOS. See ibid., at [95]. However, since UNCLOS refers to the internal waters in several provisions – albeit to a very limited extent – these waters cannot be held to *completely* fall outside of the scope of the Convention. See generally M. Kohen, 'Is the Internal Waters Regime Excluded from the United Nations Convention on the Law of the Sea?', in L. del Castillo (ed), *Law of the Sea, From Grotius to the International Tribunal for the Law of the Sea: Liber Amicorum Judge Hugo Caminos* (Brill: Leiden, 2015), 110–124. This view was explicitly endorsed with respect to Article 192 of UNCLOS in *Dispute Concerning Coastal State Rights in the Black Sea, Sea of Azov, and Kerch Strait* (n. 21), at [295].

49 See also H. Bang, 'Port State Jurisdiction and Article 218 of the UN Convention on the Law of Sea' (2009) 40 *Journal of Maritime Law and Commerce* 291, at 294: "The term 'jurisdiction' should be interpreted to mean a State's internal waters (including ports and rivers) and territorial sea".

50 Directive (EC) 2005/35 of the European Parliament and of the Council of 7 September 2005 on Ship-source Pollution and on the Introduction of Penalties for Infringements OJ L 255/11.

51 Proelß and Schatz (n. 24), at 42.

by the use of exhaust gas cleaning systems that reduce the SOx content of ship exhaust gas. SOx emissions, in turn, are covered by Annex VI of the MARPOL Convention. Also in light of the fact that this Annex contains regulations specifically applicable to exhaust gas cleaning systems, Annex VI to the MARPOL Convention must be held to prescribe *leges speciales* vis-à-vis Annexes I and IV to the MARPOL Convention, which can thus not be relied upon when assessing whether or not discharges of scrubber washwater are permissible.[52]

Annex VI to the MARPOL Convention aims to reduce air pollutants contained in ship exhaust gases, in particular SOx.[53] Regulation 14 of Annex VI to the MARPOL Convention contains emission limits for SOx and particulate matter for the use of marine fuels.[54] Thus, the primary approach taken by Annex VI to the MARPOL Convention to avoid SOx emissions is to limit the maximum sulphur content of the marine fuels used.[55]

Regulation 14 of Annex VI to the MARPOL Convention distinguishes between limits applicable within Emission Control Areas (ECAs) created for SOx and particulate matter and those applicable outside ECAs (see Table 1). Within ECAs, the limit for SOx is currently 0.1% m/m.[56] As most ships operate both inside and outside of ECAs, they must be able to comply with the respective requirements both inside and outside these areas. The North Sea and Baltic Sea are designated as ECAs.[57] Outside ECAs, a sulphur limit of 0.5% m/m came into force on 1 January 2020.[58]

In addition, Regulation 4 of Annex VI to the MARPOL Convention allows the use of *alternative procedures*, provided that they achieve a comparable limitation of emissions. These procedures include "secondary" methods such as exhaust gas cleaning systems, which, while not preventing the formation of

52 Lange, Markus and Helfst (n. 34), at 55 correctly point out that scrubber washwater may in principle also contain oil, the discharge of which is generally prohibited under Regulation 15.1 of Annex IV to the MARPOL Convention. However, it may be doubted that scrubber washwater will exceed the limits for the concentration of oil as specified in Regulation 15.2 No. 3 and 15.3 No. 3.

53 Annex VI to the MARPOL Convention (adopted in 1997, entered into force on 19 May 2005, new version in force since 1 July 2010). See also IMO, 'Prevention of Air Pollution from Ships' 2020, at: <https://www.imo.org/en/OurWork/Environment/Pages/Air-Pollution.aspx> (accessed 17 November 2020).

54 A definition of "marine fuels" can be found in Regulation 2.9 of Annex VI to the MARPOL Convention.

55 Proelß and Schatz (n. 24), at 43.

56 MARPOL Convention, Annex VI, Regulation 14.4.

57 IMO, 'Emission Control Areas (ECAs) designated under MARPOL Annex VI' 2020, at: <https://www.imo.org/en/OurWork/Environment/Pages/Emission-Control-Areas-(ECAs)-designated-under-regulation-13-of-MARPOL-Annex-VI-(NOx-emission-control).aspx> (accessed 17 November 2020).

58 MARPOL Convention, Annex VI, Regulation 14.1.3.

TABLE 1 Limits for the sulphur content of marine fuels in accordance with Regulations 14.1 and 14.4 of Annex VI to the MARPOL Convention

| SOx limits outside ECAS | SOx limits within ECAS |
|---|---|
| 4,50% m/m until 1 January 2012 | 1.50% m/m until 1 July 2010 |
| 3.50% m/m since 1 January 2012 | 1.00% m/m since 1 July 2010 |
| 0.50% m/m since 1 January 2020 | 0.10% m/m since 1 January 2015 |

pollutants, (partly) remove them from the exhaust gas through after-treatment before entering the atmosphere.[59] In the ECAS of the North and Baltic Seas, exhaust gas cleaning systems are already being used to a considerable extent because of the stricter limits. It is also to be expected that the tightening of the limits outside ECAS as of 1 January 2020 will lead to a further increase in the operation of exhaust gas cleaning systems.

Pursuant to Regulation 4.1 of Annex VI to the MARPOL Convention, Contracting Parties *may* permit the use of alternative compliance methods. However, this only applies if the operation of the methods concerned is "equivalent", i.e., at least as effective as the use of fuel oil with a sulphur content not exceeding the limits stipulated in Regulations 14.1 or 14.4 of Annex VI to the MARPOL Convention. The approval of alternative compliance methods is thus at the discretion of the Contracting Parties, provided that it is ensured that these methods are at least as effective as the use of low-sulphur marine fuels.[60] Pursuant to Regulation 4.2 of Annex VI to the MARPOL Convention, Contracting Parties which permit the use of alternative compliance must notify the relevant regulations and requirements to the IMO. Of course, Contracting Parties to the MARPOL Convention may also prohibit the use of scrubbers, whose operation requires washwater discharges, entirely.[61]

Regulation 4.1 does not explicitly specify the standard against which the effectiveness of alternative emission control methods must be measured. In this respect, the IMO has taken the view that the Contracting Parties should

59 Proelß and Schatz (n. 24), at 44.

60 Ibid.

61 For examples of State practice, see A. Honniball, 'Singapore: Precautionary Unilateralism: Port State Prohibition on Open-Loop Scrubber Discharges and the IMO 2020 Fuel Oil Sulphur Limit' (2019) 4 *Asia-Pacific Journal of Ocean Law and Policy* 270; For an example of regulation of sulphur emissions at the local level, see Y. Shi, 'China's First Local Regulation on Air Pollution from Vessels: An Appraisal' (2020) 5 *Asia-Pacific Journal of Ocean Law and Policy* 222.

take all relevant guidelines into account.[62] Specifically for secondary emission control methods, the IMO has issued updated guidelines for exhaust gas cleaning systems (Guidelines for Exhaust Gas Cleaning Systems or Guidelines) in 2015.[63] The revised Guidelines have replaced the former guidelines of the same name which were adopted in 2009.[64] Although not a legally binding document per se, the Guidelines are indirectly binding through the obligation to take them into account as codified in Regulation 4.1 of Annex VI to the MARPOL Convention.[65]

Para. 10 of the IMO Guidelines for Exhaust Gas Cleaning Systems contains instructions for the handling of scrubber washwater.[66] Para. 10.1 of the Guidelines prescribes that washwater is continuously monitored and recorded, especially when operating exhaust gas cleaning systems in ports, harbours or estuaries, but also in other areas. The monitoring and recording duties refer to the pH-value, concentration of polycyclic aromatic hydrocarbons (PAH concentration), turbidity and temperature of the water. Short interruptions for maintenance and cleaning of the equipment remain admissible.

Pursuant to para. 10.1 of the Guidelines, various limit values for the abovementioned properties of the washwater should also be observed and monitored. In this respect, the essential requirements can only be summarized here: first, the washwater discharged at the outlet of the ship should have a pH value of at least 6.5, with the exception that during manoeuvering and transit the maximum difference measured between the inlet and outlet of the ship may be 2 pH units.[67] Second, the continuous maximum concentration of PAHs in the washwater should in principle not be more than 50 μg/L PAH phenantrene equivalence in the inlet water.[68] Third, the washwater treatment system should be designed to minimize the presence of suspended particulate matter, including heavy metals and ash.[69] Fourth, the maximum continuous turbidity of the washwater should not exceed 25 formazin nephlometric units (FNU) or

62 IMO (n. 12).

63 IMO Marine Environment Protection Committee Resolution MEPC.259(68), of 15 May 2015, *Guidelines for Exhaust Gas Cleaning Systems*.

64 IMO Marine Environment Protection Committee Resolution MEPC.184(59), of 17 July 2009, *Guidelines for Exhaust Gas Cleaning Systems*.

65 Proelß and Schatz (n. 24), at 45; A. Proelß and V. J. Schatz, 'Einleitungen von Schiffsabwasser aus Abgasreinigungsanlagen: Eine rechtliche Bestandsaufnahme' (2019) 30 *Zeitschrift für Umweltrecht* 592, at 595–596.

66 A footnote in the guidelines indicates that they will be revised as soon as new scientific knowledge about the contents of the washwater and their effects becomes available.

67 Para. 10.1.2.1 of the Guidelines.

68 Para. 10.1.3.2 of the Guidelines.

69 Para. 10.1.4.2 of the Guidelines.

25 nephelometric turbidity units (NTU) or equivalent units above the turbidity of the inlet water.[70] Fifth, the washwater treatment system should prevent the discharged quantity of nitrates from being greater than the quantity associated with the 12% removal of NOx from the exhaust gas or from exceeding the normal value of nitrates of 60 mg/l for a washwater discharge rate of 45 tons/MWh, whichever is the greater.[71] For exhaust gas cleaning systems that use washwater additives and other substances or produce relevant chemicals on site, an independent assessment of the washwater is required and, if necessary, new limit values should be established by the competent authorities.[72] There are detailed requirements for the monitoring of washwater.[73] Finally, residues from exhaust gas cleaning systems (so-called sludge) are to be disposed of at suitable land-based reception facilities and thus should neither be disposed of at sea nor incinerated on board.[74] For this purpose, all ships equipped with an exhaust gas cleaning system should keep a record.

### 2.1.3 Convention on the Collection, Deposit and Reception of Waste Generated During Navigation on the Rhine and Other Inland Waterways

#### 2.1.3.1 *Objectives and Scope*

The 1996 Convention on the Collection, Deposit and Reception of Waste Generated During Navigation on the Rhine and Other Inland Waterways (CDNI)[75] aims to protect the aquatic environment and to improve safety in inland waterway transport by avoiding ship-generated waste discharges.[76] Its Contracting Parties are Belgium, France, Germany, Luxembourg, the Netherlands, and Switzerland.[77]

Pursuant to Article 2 CDNI, the geographical scope of the CDNI covers all waterways listed in its Annex 1, with extent of application to national waterways being left to the determination of the individual Contracting Parties (see Table 2). Its substantive scope covers both inland waterway vessels and

70 Para. 10.1.4.3 of the Guidelines.

71 Para. 10.1.5.1 of the Guidelines.

72 Para. 10.1.6.1 of the Guidelines.

73 Para. 10.2 of the Guidelines.

74 Paras. 10.4.1 and 10.4.2 of the Guidelines.

75 *Convention on the Collection, Deposit and Reception of Waste Generated During Navigation on the Rhine and Other Inland Waterways*, adopted 9 September 1996, entered into force 1 November 2009, Overheid Treaty Database, at: <https://treatydatabase.overheid.nl/en/Verdrag/Details/007367.html> (accessed 17 November 2020).

76 CDNI, 'The Convention' 2020, at: <https://www.cdni-iwt.org/presentation-of-cdni/?lang=en> (accessed 17 November 2020).

77 Ibid.

TABLE 2 Waterways referred to in Article 2 CDNI

| Contracting Party | Waterways |
|---|---|
| Germany | All inland waterways intended for general traffic with the exception of the German part of Lake Constance and the stretch of the Rhine upstream of Rheinfelden. |
| Belgium | All waterways accessible to inland navigation. |
| France | Part A of Annex 2 to the CDNI:<br>The Rhine, the canalised Moselle as far as Metz (km 298.5).<br>Parts B and C of Annex 2 to the CDNI:<br>The Rhine, the canalised Moselle as far as Neuves-Maisons (km 392.45), the NifferMulhouse canal, the canal between the lock at Pont Malin (km 0.0) and the border between France and Belgium (km 36.561), the widegauge canal between the lock at Pont Malin (km 0.0) and the lock at Mardyck (km 143.075), the canal between Bauvin (km 0.0) and the border between France and Belgium (km 33.850). |
| Luxembourg | The Moselle. |
| Netherlands | All waterways accessible to inland navigation. |
| Switzerland | The Rhine between Basel and Rheinfelden. |

seagoing vessels, but the latter only insofar as they operate on inland waterways.[78] Indeed, Article 1(g) of the CDNI defines a vessel as "an inland waterway vessel, seagoing vessel, or floating equipment". According to Article 1(i) of the CDNI, a seagoing vessel is a "vessel permitted to undertake maritime or coastal navigation and used principally for such navigation". Thus, if a CDNI provision refers to "vessels", it also applies to seagoing vessels unless otherwise specified.[79]

#### 2.1.3.2 *Substantive Provisions concerning Scrubber Washwater Discharges*

Article 3(1) of the CDNI prohibits the discharge of ship-generated waste from vessels, including seagoing vessels, on waterways included in the scope of the CDNI. The Contracting Parties are obliged to ensure compliance with this

78 M. Reimann, *Binnenschiffahrt, Umweltrecht und Gewässerschutz im nationalen und internationalen Kontext* (Nomos: Baden-Baden, 1999), at 52.

79 Proelß and Schatz (n. 24), at 46.

prohibition.[80] Exceptions are only permitted in accordance with Annex 2 to the CDNI.[81]

Scrubber washwater is not explicitly mentioned in the CDNI, which raises the question of whether it can be categorized as "other waste generated from the operation of the vessel" within the meaning of Article 1(e) of the CDNI and Article 8.01(e) of Annex 2, Part C, Chapter VIII to the CDNI.[82] *Prima facie*, the fact that all States Parties to the CDNI – with the exception of Germany (and possibly Belgium) – initially acted on the assumption that the CDNI did not apply to scrubber washwater[83] seems to militate against the inclusion of such washwater in the scope of "other waste generated from the operation of the vessel". In addition, it may be argued that there is generally a distinction between waste and washwater in environmental legislation. For example, Article 2(2)(a) of the EU Waste Framework Directive[84] explicitly excludes wastewater from the scope of this Directive.

On the basis of a more detailed analysis of the relevant standards of the CDNI, however, the preferable view is that scrubber washwater is included in the scope of the CDNI.[85] Article 1(e) of the CDNI defines "[o]ther waste generated from the operation of the vessel" as "domestic waste water, domestic refuse, cleansing slurry, slops and other special waste as defined in Part C of the Implementing Regulation". "Other special waste" is, again, defined in Article 8.01(e) of Annex II, Part C, Chapter VIII to the CDNI as "waste generated from the operation of the vessel other than oily and greasy waste and other than the waste referred to in sub-sections a) to d)". While the explicit inclusion of domestic wastewater as defined in Article 8.01(a) of Annex II, Part C, Chapter VIII to the CDNI in the scope of Article 1(e) of the CDNI at first sight seems to suggest that wastewater *generated by the operation of the ship* (such as scrubber washwater) is not covered by the scope of the Convention, the legal definition of the generic term "[w]aste generated from the operation of the

80 CDNI, Art. 3(2).

81 CDNI, Art. 3(3).

82 Cf. Proelß and Schatz (n. 24), at 47–49.

83 Germany is the only State Party that stated in a survey undertaken by the EU Commission that the discharge of scrubber washwater is prohibited under the CDNI. See EU Commission ENV.C.3/RH, of 18 January 2016, Commission's Views on the Discharge of Scrubber Wash Water and the Updated Table Summarising the Position of Member States on the Acceptability of Discharges of Scrubber Wash Water, Annex I. Belgium stated that scrubber washwater discharges were prohibited in inland waters and ports, but it did not make explicit reference to the CDNI.

84 Directive (EC) 2008/98 of the European Parliament and of the Council of 19 November 2008 on Waste and Repealing certain Directives OJ L 312/3.

85 See Proelß and Schatz (n. 24), at 47–49.

vessel" contained directly in Article 1(e) of the CDNI as well as Article 1(b) of the CDNI show that wastewater generated by the operation of a vessel indeed falls within the scope of the CDNI. Article 1(b) of the CDNI also clarifies that the Convention does not clearly distinguish between waste and wastewater. In addition to that, an interpretation based on the object and purpose of the CDNI militates in favour of classifying scrubber washwater as "other waste generated from the operation of the vessel" under Article 1(e) of the CDNI.[86] In view of the potential environmental risks involved, there is no reason to treat scrubber washwater differently from domestic wastewater expressly mentioned in Article 1(e) of the CDNI, or from scrubber sludge, which indisputably falls under the term waste generated from the operation of the vessel, respectively.[87] Since Article 9.01(1) of Annex II, Part C, Chapter IX to the CDNI prohibits the dumping or discharging of waste and wastewater into waterways without exception, this provision imposes an *absolute prohibition* of discharges of scrubber washwater.[88]

A different view could perhaps be taken based on the fact that on certain tankers, a so-called inerting of cargo tanks[89] is required to meet the rules of Regulations 4.5.5.1.2 and 4.5.5.3.2 of Chapter II-2 of the Convention for the Safety of Life at Sea (SOLAS)[90] in conjunction with paras. 2.3.1.3.1 and 2.3.1.5 of Chapter 15 of the International Code for Fire Safety Systems (FSS Code).[91] The FSS Code is an IMO Code that is binding by virtue of Chapter II-2 of the Annex to the SOLAS Convention (in the present context by Regulation 4.5.5.1.2). If inerting is carried out with flue gas, as it is usually done on oil tankers, para. 2.3.1.3.1 of Chapter 15 of the FSS Code requires the gas to be cooled and sulphur compounds to be washed out by a scrubber. During the operation of inert gas installations using flue gas, the resulting scrubber washwater is

86 CDNI, 'Résidus de Curage et Gaz Inertes' 2020, at: <https://www.cdni-iwt.org/faq/divers/> (accessed 17 November 2020). See also CDNI, 'Guide CDNI: Pour l'application des dispositions relatives à l'élimination des déchets et à l'utilisation de produits de nettoyage conformément à la CDNI' 2016, at: <https://www.cdni-iwt.org/wp-content/uploads/2016/01/Brochure-CDNI-nettoyage-2016-FR.pdf> (accessed 17 November 2020), 5.

87 Proelß and Schatz (n. 24), at 47.

88 Consenting CDNI (n. 86).

89 Inerting ensures that the atmosphere of the cargo tanks cannot ignite. See IMO Maritime Safety Committee Resolution MSC.98(73), of 5 December 2000, *The International Code for Fire Safety Systems*, Annex, No. 2.2.1.1. Chapter 15 of the FSS Code was last replaced by IMO Maritime Safety Committee Resolution MSC.367(93), of 22 May 2014, *Amendments to the International Code for Fire Safety Systems (FSS Code)*.

90 *Convention for the Safety of Life at Sea*, adopted 1 November 1974, entered into force 25 May 1980, 1184 UNTS 278.

91 See also CDNI (n. 86).

usually discharged into the water. Against this background, a restrictive interpretation of the scope of the CDNI could be considered in the light of the mandatory requirements of the FSS Code in order to avoid conflicting legal requirements.[92] However, it should be noted that, although the FSS Code itself does not impose any restrictions on the handling of scrubber washwater, it does not legally require that washwater generated by the operation of the scrubbers used on the ships concerned be discharged into the aquatic environment.[93] On closer inspection, this means that strictly speaking no conflict between the FSS Code and the CDNI exists.[94] As the law stands at present, the prohibition of discharges under the CDNI must thus be complied with even within the scope of the FSS Code, and this should be done by suitable technical measures to prevent the discharge of scrubber washwater.[95] Alternatively, the States Parties to the CDNI could seek to supplement Article 8.02 of Annex 2, Part C, Chapter VIII of the CNDI with regard to scrubber washwater within the framework of the Conference of the Parties.

### 2.2 *EU Legislation on the Discharge of Scrubber Washwater*

#### 2.2.1 Sulphur Directive

##### 2.2.1.1 *Objective and Scope*

At the level of EU law, the use of SOx scrubbers is primarily regulated by Directive (EU) 2016/802 concerning a Reduction in the Sulphur Content of Certain Liquid Fuels (Sulphur Directive).[96] According to its Recitals 20–26, the Sulphur Directive primarily serves to implement the obligations of EU Member States to reduce SOx emissions laid down in Annex VI to the MARPOL Convention. It applies to the use of petroleum-derived liquid fuels "within Member States' territory, territorial seas, exclusive economic zones or pollution control zones".[97]

The Sulphur Directive does not define the terms "territory" and "territorial seas". Both categories – territory and territorial seas – refer to areas which are part of the sovereign territory of the Member States and thus subject to their

92 Cf. the discussion by Proelß and Schatz (n. 24), at 48–49.

93 Ibid., at 49.

94 Ibid.

95 Ibid.

96 Directive (EU) 2016/802 of the European Parliament and of the Council of 11 May 2016 concerning a Reduction in the Sulphur Content of Certain Liquid Fuels OJ L 132/58. The provisions of the current Sulphur Directive that are relevant for scrubbers are essentially identical to those of Directive (EU) 2012/33 of the European Parliament and of the Council of 21 November 2012 Amending Council Directive 1999/32/EC as Regards the Sulphur Content of Marine Fuels OJ L 327/1. For discussion, see generally Solf (n. 7).

97 Sulphur Directive, Art. 1(2).

sovereignty. A distinction based on the terminology used in a law of the sea-related context would suggest that "territory" covers the mainland including inland and internal waters, whereas the term "territorial seas" refers to the territorial sea as referred to in Article 2(1) of UNCLOS.[98] If, in the context of the Sulphur Directive, the territorial sea were assigned to the territory, there would be no need for a separate category of "territorial seas". To assume that the internal waters do not form part of the territorial seas (as understood by the Sulphur Directive) does not contradict the inclusion of the internal waters into the scope of Annex VI to the MARPOL Convention (which the Sulphur Directive implements on the level of EU law), as the Sulphur Directive contains special rules applicable to ports (which usually form part of the internal waters).

The EEZ as referred to in Article 1(2) of the Sulphur Directive is a well-recognized concept of the international law of the sea as reflected in Part V of UNCLOS. It does not belong to the territory of the coastal State and is therefore not subject to its sovereignty. However, within that zone coastal States have been allocated exclusive and functionally limited sovereign rights and jurisdiction relating, *inter alia*, to the protection and preservation of the marine environment (cf. Article 56(1)(b)(iii) of UNCLOS).[99] Finally, "pollution control zones" within the meaning of Article 1(2) of the Sulphur Directive are areas included in Annex III of the 1999 Protocol to Abate Acidification, Eutrophication and Ground-Level Ozone[100] to the 1979 Convention on Long-range Transboundary Air Pollution[101] (cf. Article 1 No. 14 of the Protocol).

#### 2.2.1.2 *Substantive Requirements*

Representing the EU's legislative implementation of Annex VI to the MARPOL Convention, the EU Sulphur Directive prescribes maximum permitted sulphur contents in marine fuels as the primary instrument for reducing SOx emissions, but also provides for alternative emission abatement methods. EU Member States are obliged to ensure that marine fuels with a sulphur content exceeding 3.50% by mass are not used on their territories unless alternative emission abatement methods operating in closed mode are applied in accordance with Article 8 of the Sulphur Directive.[102]

98 Proelß and Schatz (n. 24), at 50.

99 Proelss, 'Article 56', in Proelss (ed.) (n. 20), 418, at [20–21].

100 *Protocol to the 1979 Convention on Long-range Transboundary Air Pollution to Abate Acidification, Eutrophication and Ground-level Ozone*, adopted 30 November 1999, entered into force 17 May 2005, 2319 UNTS 81.

101 *Convention on Long-range Transboundary Air Pollution*, adopted 13 November 1979, entered into force 16 March 1983, 1302 UNTS 217.

102 Sulphur Directive, Art. 5.

TABLE 3 Limit values for the sulphur content of marine fuels according to the Sulphur Directive

| SOx limit in territory | SOx limit in territorial seas, EEZs and pollution control zones (outside ECAs) | SOx limits in territorial seas, EEZs and pollution control zones (within ECAs) | SOx limits at berths in ports |
|---|---|---|---|
| 3,50% | 0,50% | 0,10% | 0,10% |

In addition, EU Member States have an obligation to take all necessary measures to ensure that no marine fuels with a sulphur content exceeding 0.50% by mass are used in their territorial seas, EEZ and pollution control zones, and on ships on regular service to or from a port of the EU as of 1 January 2020.[103] Insofar as the aforementioned zones are located inside of an ECA established in accordance with Annex VI to the MARPOL Convention (i.e., also in the North Sea or Baltic Sea),[104] the limit value was 1.00% of mass until 31 December 2014,[105] and since 1 January 2015 it has been 0.10% of mass.[106] At berths in ports of the EU which are part of the territory within the meaning of Article 5 of the Sulphur Directive, the limit value is 0.10 per cent by mass.[107] The Sulphur Directive thus essentially implements the limit values laid down in Regulations 14.1 and 14.4 of Annex VI to the MARPOL Convention.

However, according to Article 8(1) of the Sulphur Directive, Member States "shall allow" the use of emission abatement methods "as an alternative to using marine fuels that meet the requirements of Articles 6 and 7", provided that certain conditions are met. This applies to "ships of all flags" in "ports, territorial seas, exclusive economic zones and pollution control zones".[108] In view of the fact that the term "port" cannot be held to apply only to seaports located at the coasts of the EU Member States, Article 8(1) of the Sulphur Directive also applies to inland ports served by seagoing vessels. In contrast, inland waterways leading to ports that are called at by seagoing vessels (which equally

103 Sulphur Directive, Art. 6(1)(b).
104 The Sulphur Directive refers in this respect to "SOx Emission Control Areas", which are defined in Article 2(h) as the "Marine Areas designated as such by the [IMO] in Annex VI to the MARPOL Convention".
105 Sulphur Directive, Art. 6(2)(a).
106 Sulphur Directive, Art. 6(2)(b).
107 Sulphur Directive, Art. 7.
108 Sulphur Directive, Art. 8(1).

constitute internal waters) are arguably covered by Article 5 of the Sulphur Directive, which means that only those alternative emission abatement methods which operate in closed mode (and thus do not lead to discharges of washwater) can lawfully be operated there.

The Sulphur Directive defines the term "emission abatement method" as "any fitting, material, appliance or apparatus to be fitted in a ship or other procedure, alternative fuel, or compliance method, used as an alternative to low sulphur marine fuel meeting the requirements set out in this Directive, that is verifiable, quantifiable and enforceable".[109] The wording "shall allow" creates an *obligation* for EU Member States to establish a legal basis in their domestic law for permitting emission abatement methods that meet the above conditions.[110] In doing so, Article 8(1) of the Sulphur Directive does not contradict Regulation 4 of Annex VI to the MARPOL Convention, which grants the Contracting Parties *discretion* with regard to the domestic approval of such processes.[111] Rather, the EU has – unwittingly or not – exercised the discretion allocated to its Member States by Regulation 4 of Annex VI to the MARPOL Convention by creating a legal obligation for the Member States under EU law to allow emission abatement methods if the conditions set out in the Directive are met.[112] It remains to be analyzed whether EU Member States are nonetheless entitled to enact stricter environmental measures than those foreseen by the Sulphur Directive by directly or indirectly prohibiting the use of certain emission abatement methods (for example, by establishing an absolute prohibition on the discharge of scrubber washwater) on the basis of Article 193 of the TFEU ("more stringent protective measures").[113]

109 Sulphur Directive, Art. 2(o). See also Sulphur Directive, 34th Recital: "Access to emission abatement methods should be facilitated. Those methods can provide emission reductions at least equivalent to, or even greater than, those achievable using low sulphur fuel, provided that they have no significant negative impacts on the environment, such as marine ecosystems, and that they are developed subject to appropriate approval and control mechanisms. The already known alternative methods, such as the use of on-board exhaust gas cleaning systems, the mixture of fuel and liquefied natural gas or the use of biofuels should be recognised in the Union. It is important to promote the testing and development of new emission abatement methods in order, among other reasons, to limit modal shift from sea to land-based transport".

110 The implementation of the Sulphur Directive should also be ensured by "effective, proportionate and dissuasive sanctions", including fines. Cf. Sulphur Directive, 43th Recital.

111 See supra 2.1.2.2.

112 Under Art. 4(2)(e) of the Treaty on the Functioning of the European Union OJ C 326/47 (TFEU), the EU has shared legislative powers in the field of "environment", which it can exercise on the basis of Article 192 of the TFEU.

113 See infra 2.3.

TABLE 4 Equivalent emission values applicable to emission abatement methods pursuant to Article 8(2) of the Sulphur Directive

| Sulphur content of marine fuels (% m/m) | $SO_2$ emissions ratio (ppm)/$CO_2$ (% v/v) |
|---|---|
| 3,50 | 151,7 |
| 1,50 | 65,0 |
| 1,00 | 43,3 |
| 0,50 | 21,77 |
| 0,10 | 4,3 |

According to the Sulphur Directive, emission abatement methods may only be permitted if three conditions are met.[114] First, Article 8(2) of the Sulphur Directive requires that emission abatement methods "shall continuously achieve reductions of sulphur dioxide emissions that are at least equivalent to the reductions that would be achieved by using [low sulphur] marine fuels". This standard corresponds to that of Regulation 4 of Annex VI to the MARPOL Convention. Corresponding emission values are laid down in Annex I of the Sulphur Directive, which makes explicit reference to Regulations 14.1 and 14.4 of Annex VI to the MARPOL Convention (see Table 4). These requirements thus serve to ensure the reduction of SOx emissions from ship exhaust gases and contain specifications for exhaust gas cleaning systems as such, but not for scrubber washwater.

Second, emission abatement methods must meet further criteria laid down in Annex II of the Sulphur Directive, which also apply to washwater from exhaust gas cleaning systems, in order to be permitted under Article 8(4) of the Sulphur Directive. In this respect, Annex II of the Sulphur Directive refers to the 2009 version of the IMO Guidelines for Exhaust Gas Cleaning Systems.[115] These requirements should also be considered in the light of the prohibition

114 The approval of emission abatement methods for the use on board ships flying the flag of an EU Member State (but not onboard ships flying the flag of third countries) is conducted in accordance with Art. 9 of the Sulphur Directive.

115 Note that the 2015 version of the IMO Guidelines had already been adopted when the Sulphur Directive was enacted. See supra 2.1.2.2. Arguably, the fact that the Sulphur Dorective refers in its Annex II to an outdated version of the IMO Guidelines does not affect the binding nature of the standards contained therein within the framework of the Directive.

under Article 195 of UNCLOS, of transformation of one type of the pollution into another.[116]

Third, Annex II of the Sulphur Directive provides for a prohibition, subject to permission, of the discharge of washwater from exhaust gas cleaning systems which use "chemicals, additives, preparations and relevant chemicals created *in situ*" as defined in para. 10.1.6.1 of the Guidelines for Exhaust Gas Cleaning Systems of 2009. Such washwater may not be discharged "into the sea, including enclosed ports, harbours and estuaries, unless it is demonstrated by the ship operator that such washwater discharge has no significant negative impacts on and does not pose risks to human health and the environment". The need for permission does not refer to the actual discharge of the washwater, but to the approval of the emission abatement methods in accordance with Article 9 of the Sulphur Directive.[117] The terms "significant negative impacts" and "risks" used by Annex II of the Sulphur Directive are not defined, which leaves EU Member States considerable leeway in adopting more specific regulation with respect to scrubber washwater discharges.[118] Depending on how the requirements for the proof of compliance with the current and future standards are set by the EU Member States, the requirements imposed can represent a considerable hurdle for operators of exhaust gas cleaning systems, especially in view of the insufficient scientific knowledge about the potentially adverse environmental effects of scrubber washwater.[119] With this prohibition, the Sulphur Directive implements the Guidelines for Exhaust Gas Cleaning Systems, which in turn require a separate check when using "wash water additives and other substances", as no limit values have yet been standardized for such substances. Only when an exhaust gas cleaning system uses caustic soda as a chemical, it is sufficient that the washwater: (1) complies with the 2009 Guidelines for Exhaust Gas Cleaning Systems; and (2) the pH value of the washwater does not exceed 8.0. According to para. 10.1.2.1 of the Guidelines, the lower limit is a pH value of 6.5, which means that the pH value of the washwater must be between 6.5 and 8.0.[120] The pH value of 8.0 is close to the pH value of sea water.[121] In this respect, the EU has already imposed stricter requirements for

116 See supra 2.1.1.

117 This is due to the fact that the Sulphur Directive does not provide for a permit for the individual discharge itself.

118 Proelß and Schatz (n. 24), at 53–54.

119 Markus and Helfst (n. 23), at 765 raise the possibility that the requirements might have a prohibitive effect. See Proelß and Schatz (n. 24), at 53–54.

120 For the further requirements of the Guidelines, see supra 2.1.2.2. The current version of the Guidelines contains a corresponding provision in para. 10.1.2.

121 According to a report of the Royal Society, the surface water of the oceans has a global average pH value of 8.2. See Royal Society, 'Ocean Acidification Due to Increasing

a specific type of "wash water additives and other substances" (namely those using caustic soda as a chemical).[122]

### 2.2.2 Directive on Port Reception Facilities

In addition to the provisions of the Sulphur Directive, the Directive (EU) 2019/883 on Port Reception Facilities for the Delivery of Waste from Ships (Directive on Port Reception Facilities)[123] is relevant in the context of sludge and washwater discharges resulting from the operation of (closed) exhaust gas cleaning systems. According to its Article 1, the main objective of this Directive is "to protect the marine environment against the negative effects from discharges of waste from ships using ports located in the [EU]" by "improving the availability and use of adequate port reception facilities and the delivery of waste to those facilities".[124] The Directive aims to achieve this goal by obliging EU Member States to ensure the availability of such port reception facilities.[125] In principle, Member States shall ensure that all ship-generated waste falling within the scope of the Directive is disposed of as provided under the Directive.[126] Before departure, masters of ships calling at EU ports are required to deliver all waste carried on board to a port reception facility in accordance with the applicable discharge norms pursuant to the MARPOL Convention.[127] Thus, the Directive on Port Reception Facilities can be regarded as another instrument by which the EU has implemented parts of the MARPOL Convention and its Annexes.[128]

In view of para. 10.4.2 of the 2015 IMO Guidelines for Exhaust Gas Cleaning Systems of 2015, it is necessary that suitable port reception facilities for scrubber sludge and washwater are provided in EU ports. In contrast to its earlier version,[129] the new Directive on Port Reception Facilities now applies to these

---

Atmospheric Carbon Dioxide' (2005), at: <https://royalsociety.org/~/media/Royal_Society_Content/policy/publications/2005/9634.pdf> (accessed 17 November 2020), 6.

122 Proelß and Schatz (n. 24), at 54.

123 Directive (EU) 2019/883 of the European Parliament and of the Council of 17 April 2019 on Port Reception Facilities for the Delivery of Waste from Ships, Amending Directive (EU) 2010/65 and Repealing Directive 2000/59/EC OJ L 151/116.

124 According to Art. 2(6) of the Directive, port reception facilities "means any facility which is fixed, floating or mobile and capable of providing the service of receiving the waste from ships".

125 Directive on Port Reception Facilities, Art. 4(1).

126 Ibid., Art. 3(2).

127 Ibid., Art. 7(1).

128 See ibid., Preamble, 3rd to 6th Recital. Note that the new Directive is expressly provided for bringing EU law in line with the latest amendments to Annex VI to the MARPOL Convention (Preamble, 6th Recital), and to eliminate "inconsistencies with the MARPOL Convention framework" (Preamble, 12th Recital).

129 For discussion see Proelß and Schatz (n. 24), at 53–54.

types of waste. The definition of the term "waste from ships" covers "all waste, including cargo residues, which is generated during the service of a ship or during loading, unloading and cleaning operations and which falls within the scope of Annexes I, II, IV, V and VI to the MARPOL Convention, as well as passively fished waste".[130] The express reference to Annex VI to the MARPOL Convention clarifies that sludge and scrubber washwater are indeed included within the scope of the new Directive,[131] and that the regulatory gap which existed prior to the entry into force of the 2019 Directive[132] was, as had been demanded by the Commission's Explanatory Memorandum to the proposed a new version of the Directive on Port Reception Facilities,[133] closed.

In all this, it should be added that the Preamble of the Directive on Port Reception Facilities calls upon the Member States to continue to work at the IMO "for a comprehensive consideration of the environmental impacts of wastewater discharges from open loop scrubbers, including for measures to counter possible impacts" and encourages them "to take appropriate measures in accordance with Directive 2000/60/EC of the European Parliament and of the Council [the Water Framework Directive],[134] including discharge bans for wastewater from open loop scrubbers and certain cargo residues in their territorial waters".[135] While the call for further considering the environmental impacts of wastewater discharges from open loop scrubbers in the context of the IMO can essentially be traced back to the precautionary principle and thus

130 Directive on Port Reception Facilities, Art. 2(3). Art. 2(4) of the Directive defines "passively fished waste" as "waste collected in nets during fishing operations".

131 See also the amended definition of "cargo residues" in Directive on Port Reception Facilities, Art. 2(5): "'cargo residues' means the remnants of any cargo material on board which remain on the deck or in holds or tanks following loading and unloading, including loading and unloading excess or spillage, whether in wet or dry condition *or entrained in wash-water*, excluding cargo dust remaining on the deck after sweeping or dust of the external surfaces of the ship" (italics added).

132 EU Commission COM(2018) 188, of 16 April 2018, Report from the Commission to the European Parliament and the Council on Implementation and Compliance with the Sulphur Standards for Marine Fuels Set Out in Directive (EU) 2016/802 Relating to a Reduction in the Sulphur Content of Certain Liquid Fuels, 12: "To further reduce the negative impacts of EGCS on the marine environment and to ensure alignment with MARPOL Annex VI, the Commission recently proposed to include the residues and bleed-off water from EGCS as waste types in its proposal for a 'new' Directive on Port Reception Facilities for the delivery of waste from ships".

133 EU Commission COM(2018) 33 final, of 16 January 2018, Proposal for a Directive of the European Parliament and of the Council on Port Reception Facilities for Ship-generated waste, repealing Directive 2000/59/EC and amending Directives 2009/16/EC and 2010/65/EU, 10.

134 See the discussion infra 2.2.4.

135 Directive on Port Reception Facilities, Preamble, 7th and 8th Recital.

deserves full approval, the express reference to discharge bans for wastewater from open loop scrubbers is somewhat surprising, considering that the EU, by adopting the Sulphur Directive, has specified the requirements of Annex VI to the MARPOL Convention[136] by establishing a general obligation to authorize the operation of emission abatement methods such as open loop scrubbers.[137]

### 2.2.3 Marine Strategy Framework Directive

#### 2.2.3.1 *Objectives and Scope*

The purpose of Directive (EC) 2008/56 Establishing a Framework for Community Action in the Field of Marine Environmental Policy (MSFD)[138] is to establish a framework within which EU Member States are obliged to take the necessary measures to achieve or maintain a good environmental status in the marine environment by 2020 at the latest.[139] In 2020, the European Commission published a report on the implementation of the MSFD, concluding that "progress in reaching good environmental status has not been fast enough to cover all MSFD descriptors in all EU waters by 2020" and identifying "critical areas for improvement" in the future.[140]

The scope of the MSFD covers all "marine waters",[141] which include parts of the internal waters,[142] the territorial sea, the continental shelf and the EEZ as defined in UNCLOS.[143] The Directive is based on the ecosystem approach. Its aim is to ensure that overall pressures from anthropogenic activities are limited to levels consistent with the achievement of a good environmental status, and that the capacity of marine ecosystems to respond to human-induced changes is not impaired, while at the same time allowing for the sustainable use of marine goods and services by present and future generations.[144] Within

136 See supra 2.1.2.2.

137 See supra 2.2.1.2.

138 Directive (EC) 2008/56 of the European Parliament and of the Council of 17 June 2018 Establishing a Framework for Community Action in the Field of Marine Environmental Policy OJ L 164/19.

139 MSFD, Art. 1(1).

140 EU Commission COM(2020) 259 final, of 25 June 2020, Report from the Commission to the European Parliament and the Council on the Implementation of the Marine Strategy Framework Directive (Directive 2008/56/EC), at 29–30.

141 MSFD, Art. 2(1).

142 This follows from Article 2(1) in conjunction with Article 3 No. 1(b) of the MSFD.

143 Article 2(1) in conjunction with Article 3 No. 1(a) MSFD. See A. Proelß, 'Article 43 WHG', in M. Beckmann, W. Durner, T. Mann et al. (eds.), *Landmann/Rohmer: Umweltrecht: Kommentar (92nd ed.)* (C. H. Beck: Munich, 2020), [18–21]; A. Proelß, '§ 45a WHG', in M. Beckmann, W. Durner, T. Mann et al. (eds.), *Landmann/Rohmer: Umweltrecht: Kommentar (92nd ed.)* (C. H. Beck: Munich, 2020), [17].

144 MSFD, Art. 1(3).

this framework, the MSFD is also (generally) relevant to the issue of the permissibility of discharges of scrubber washwater.[145]

#### 2.2.3.2 *Regulatory Approach*

The MSFD does not itself directly regulate standards for achieving a good environmental status of the marine environment, nor does it address the issue of whether a specific use of marine waters is subject to authorization. Rather, it requires Member States to develop and implement marine strategies to achieve a good environmental status.[146] Pursuant to Article 5(1) of the MSFD, EU Member States must thus develop marine strategies for the marine regions and subregions listed in Article 4 of the MSFD in respect of marine areas under their jurisdiction up to the outer limits of the EEZ and continental shelf in order to achieve the objective of achieving good status of the marine environment by 2020 as laid down in Article 1 of the MSFD.[147] These strategies must "protect and preserve the marine environment, prevent its deterioration or, where practicable, restore marine ecosystems in areas where they have been adversely affected".[148] They shall also aim to prevent and reduce inputs into the marine environment in order to progressively eliminate pollution.[149]

In accordance with Article 5(2) of the MSFD, the procedure (so-called plan of action) for developing marine strategies is divided into six steps, which in turn are assigned to two phases – that of preparation and that of programmes of measures. Preparation[150] comprises (1) an initial assessment to determine the current environmental status of the waters in question and the impact of human activity on the environmental status of these waters,[151] (2) a description of their good environmental status,[152] (3) the establishment of environmental targets and associated indicators,[153] and (4) the establishment and implementation of a monitoring programme for the ongoing assessment and regular updating of the objectives of the strategy targets.[154] The phase of programmes of measures[155] is divided into (1) the development of a programme of measures

145 Cf. Lange, Markus and Helfst (n. 34), at 57–58; Proelß and Schatz (n. 24), at 56.
146 Cf. MSFD, Art. 1(2). See Lange, Markus and Helfst (n 34), at 57, with further references.
147 Proelß and Schatz (n. 24), at 56.
148 MSFD, Art. 1(2)(a).
149 MSFD, Art. 1(2)(b).
150 MSFD, Art. 5(2)(a).
151 MSFD, Art. 5(2)(a)(i).
152 MSFD, Art. 5(2)(a)(ii).
153 MSFD, Art. 5(2)(a)(iii).
154 MSFD, Art. 5(2)(a)(iv).
155 MSFD, Art. 5(2)(b).

designed to achieve or maintain good environmental status[156] and (2) the entry into operation of this programme.[157] All steps must be completed within the timeframe specified by Article 5(2) of the MSFD. Descriptor 8 of Annex I of the MSFD, according to which no pollution effect should result from concentrations of pollutants, is particularly relevant for the discharge of scrubber washwater.[158] This descriptor is to be considered when establishing good environmental status in a marine region or subregion pursuant to Article 9(1) of the MSFD.

Pollution is defined under the MSFD as "the direct or indirect introduction into the marine environment, as a result of human activity, of substances or energy, […] which results or is likely to result in deleterious effects such as harm to living resources and marine ecosystems, […], including loss of biodiversity, hazards to human health, the hindering of marine activities, including fishing, tourism and recreation and other legitimate uses of the sea, impairment of the quality for use of sea water and reduction of amenities or, in general, impairment of the sustainable use of marine goods and services".[159] Due to the breadth of this definition, scrubber washwater constitutes pollution if it can be shown to have any (even the smallest) negative impact on the marine environment.[160] As stated, the MSFD itself does not prohibit pollution, but only obliges EU Member States to implement the Directive's objectives through the development of marine strategies.[161] Therefore, a prohibition on the discharge of scrubber washwater can only result from national legislation implementing the MSFD, not from the Directive itself.[162]

### 2.2.4 Water Framework Directive

#### 2.2.4.1 *Objectives and Scope*

Directive (EC) 2000/60 Establishing a Framework for Community Action in the Field of Water Policy (WFD)[163] aims to "establish a framework for the protection of inland surface waters, transitional waters, coastal waters and groundwater" that, *inter alia*, "prevents further deterioration and protects

156 MSFD, Art. 5(2)(b)(i).
157 MSFD, Art. 5(2)(b)(ii).
158 MSFD, Annex I. See also the comments by Lange, Markus and Helfst (n. 54), at 57–58.
159 MSFD, Art. 3(8).
160 Proelß and Schatz (n. 24), at 57.
161 Ibid.
162 Ibid.
163 Directive (EC) 2000/60 of the European Parliament and of the Council of 23 October 2000 Establishing a Framework for Community Action in the Field of Water Policy OJ L 327/1.

and enhances the status of aquatic ecosystems",[164] "promotes sustainable water use based on a long-term protection of available water resources",[165] "aims at enhanced protection and improvement of the aquatic environment",[166] "ensures the progressive reduction of pollution of groundwater and prevents its further pollution",[167] and "contributes to mitigating the effects of floods and droughts".[168] In order to achieve these general objectives, the WFD pursues an "integrated Community policy on water",[169] taking into account "qualitative and quantitative aspects" and "the natural flow conditions of water"[170] within the water cycle through coordinated "measures in respect of surface water and groundwaters belonging to the same ecological, hydrological and hydrogeological system".[171] The core objective of the WFD is to achieve at least "good water status" of surface waters in the EU.[172] As stated by Article 4(1) of the WFD, this general environmental quality objective is further developed by environmental objectives tailored to the specific requirements of different categories of surface water.

In addition to groundwater, the WFD applies to surface water, which includes "inland waters, [...] transitional waters and coastal waters".[173] Coastal waters within the meaning of the WFD are "surface water on the landward side of a line, every point of which is at a distance of one nautical mile on the seaward side from the nearest point of the baseline from which the breadth of territorial waters is measured, extending where appropriate up to the outer limit of transitional waters".[174] This definition does not correspond to the definition of the territorial sea in terms of UNCLOS.[175] Therefore, "surface waters" in terms of the WFD do not include most of the territorial sea, the EEZ and the continental shelf, but cover the internal waters (including inland waterways and inland seaports) and inland waters.[176] However, Article 2(1) of the WFD makes clear by way of exception that, with regard to the chemical status of the waters

164 WFD, Art. 1(a).
165 WFD, Art. 1(b).
166 WFD, Art. 1(c).
167 WFD, Art. 1(d).
168 WFD, Art. 1(e).
169 WFD, Preamble, 9th Recital.
170 WFD, Preamble, 34th Recital.
171 WFD, Preamble, 33rd Recital.
172 WFD, Preamble, 25th and 26th Recital.
173 WFD, Art. 2(1).
174 WFD, Art. 2(7).
175 Proelß (n. 143), at [22].
176 Proelß and Schatz (n. 24), at 58.

concerned, the term "territorial waters" indeed fully covers the territorial sea as defined under the international law of the sea.

#### 2.2.4.2 *Regulatory Approach*

To achieve its objectives, the WFD provides a framework for action in which measures to protect bodies of surface water must be coordinated, integrated and developed over the long term.[177] As far as the status of surface water is concerned, the WFD stipulates both what has been described as a "prohibition of deterioration"[178] and an "imperative for improvement".[179] Both of these concepts can be applied to the discharge of scrubber washwater. The legally binding nature of the environmental objectives codified in Article 4 of the WFD (including the above-mentioned commandments) is meanwhile beyond question. With regard to the prohibition of deterioration, the Court of Justice of the European Union (CJEU) decided in its judgment on the deepening of the River Weser that "Member States are required – unless a derogation is granted – to refuse authorisation for an individual project where it may cause a deterioration of the status of a body of surface water or where it jeopardises the attainment of good surface water status or of good ecological potential and good surface water chemical status by the date laid down by the directive".[180]

Based on the imperative for improvement of water quality, EU Member States are obliged to achieve "good surface water status"[181] in ecological and chemical terms, at the latest 15 years after the entry into force of the WFD, i.e., by 22 December 2015.[182] "Good ecological status" refers to the quality of the structure and functioning of aquatic ecosystems associated with bodies of surface water, as classified in accordance with certain criteria.[183] The scientific specification and classification of the "ecological status" of the various surface water categories is based on detailed quality criteria ("quality elements"), which relate to biological (composition and abundance of the aquatic flora and fauna), hydromorphological (e.g., water balance and navigability of rivers) and chemical or physico-chemical water properties (river basin specific pollutants, visibility depth, temperature conditions, oxygen balance, salinity, acidification status,

177 WFD, 18th Recital.
178 WFD, Art. 4(1)(a)(i).
179 WFD, Art. 4(1)(a)(ii).
180 Judgment of the CJEU in Case C-461/13 *Bund für Umwelt und Naturschutz v Germany* [51].
181 Cf. WFD, Art. 2(18).
182 WFD, Art. 4(1)(a)(ii).
183 WFD, Art. 2(21) and (22) in conjunction with Annex V.

nutrient conditions).[184] A surface water has achieved "good chemical status"[185] if it does not exceed any of the concentrations of pollutants[186] laid down in more specific legislation.[187] In this context, the WFD provides for numerous options for exemptions, ranging from extended implementation deadlines to weaker environmental quality requirements.[188] In particular, the 15-year deadline for achieving the environmental objectives can be extended by up to 12 years – i.e. until 22 December 2027 – due to technical difficulties, "disproportionate costs" or natural conditions.[189] In the opinion of the EU Commission, EU Member States have made too extensive use of these exceptions, and often without good reason.[190] In 2015, almost 50% of bodies of surface water in the EU were not in good ecological status.[191]

### 2.2.5 Relationship between Applicable EU Directives

As regards the (horizontal) relationship between the relevant Directives,[192] it may first of all be stated that there is no apparent conflict between the MSFD and the WFD. The MSFD also grants EU Member States sufficient discretion to design their marine environmental policies in such a way that they do not conflict with the Sulphur Directive. The Sulphur Directive places the discharge of scrubber washwater under a prohibition subject to permission and thus does not require that an absolute prohibition be implemented. Conversely, discharges of scrubber washwater do not necessarily violate the MSFD. Therefore, the requirements of the Sulphur Directive must be complied with in the context of implementing the MSFD. It follows that a potential future tightening of the MARPOL Convention's requirements and the implementation of these requirements in the Sulphur Directive would have to be taken into account in the implementation of the MSFD.

---

184 WFD, Annex V, No. 1.1.

185 WFD, Art. 16(7) and WFD, Annexes IX and X.

186 WFD, Art. 2(24), in particular in connection with WFD, Art. 16(7) as well as Annex IX (emission limit values and environmental quality standards) and Annex X (priority substances).

187 See, for example, Directive (EU) 2013/39 of the European Parliament and of the Council of 12 August 2013 Amending Directives 2000/60/EC and 2008/105/EC as regards Priority Substances in the Field of Water Policy OJ L 226/1.

188 WFD, Art. 4(4)–(7).

189 WFD, Art. 4(4)(a)(i)–(iii) and Art. 4(4)(c) in conjunction with Art. 13(7).

190 EU Commission COM(2015) 120, of 9 March 2015, Communication from the Commission to the European Parliament and the Council, The Water Framework Directive and the Floods Directive: Actions Towards the 'Good Status' of EU Water and to Reduce Flood Risks, at 3, 6.

191 Ibid., at 3.

192 For discussion see Proelß and Schatz (n. 24), at 59.

However, it cannot be excluded that the discharge of scrubber washwater could violate the prohibition of deterioration under the WFD to the extent that such discharges are permitted under the Sulphur Directive within the spatial scope of the WFD.[193] In this case, the regime of the WFD could collide with that of the Sulphur Directive, as the latter only stipulates a prohibition subject to permission rather than an absolute prohibition similar to that of the WFD. When implementing the Sulphur Directive, care must thus be taken to ensure that the requirements of the WFD are not disregarded.[194] The fact that the Sulphur Directive is both more recent and more specific than the WFD does arguably not affect the interpretation proposed here. According to Recital 34 of the Sulphur Directive, the use of exhaust gas cleaning systems is only desirable "provided that their use results in equivalent or even greater emission reductions and that all relevant conditions set in the Directive are fulfilled".[195] In other words, the Sulphur Directive must be interpreted and applied in such a way that it does not run counter to the general environmental protection objectives of the EU, particularly with regard to marine ecosystems.[196]

It is submitted that a conflict between the WFD and the Sulphur Directive can be avoided through a harmonizing interpretation at the level of EU law. Pursuant to Article 8(1) in conjunction with Annex II of the Sulphur Directive, a permit may only be granted if it is demonstrated by the "operator of the ship that such washwater discharge has no significant negative impacts on and does not pose risks to human health and the environment". As these requirements are not defined or further specified in the Sulphur Directive, they can serve as starting point for a harmonizing interpretation of the Sulphur Directive that ensures compliance with the requirements of the WFD. In accordance with this interpretation, EU Member States must impose requirements for discharges of scrubber washwater that simultaneously fulfill the requirements of the WFD.[197] In this respect, it should be noted that, in implementing the WFD,

193 The data situation is still unclear in this respect. See EU Commission ENV C.3/RH (n. 83), at 2; EU Parliament E-003307/2017, of 30 June 2017, Parliamentary Questions: Answer given by Mr Vella on behalf of the Commission to a Parliamentary Question posed by Jan Huitema on 2 June 2015.

194 Cf. EU Commission COM(2018) 188 (n. 132), at 14. Generally on the priority of the WFD, but without reference to the Sulphur Directive, Markus and Helfst (n. 23), at 768.

195 EU Commission COM(2018) 188 (n. 132), at 11.

196 EU Commission ENV.C.3/RH (n. 83), at 1–2; EU Parliament E-003307/2017 (n. 193): "The provisions of the Sulphur Directive […] are without prejudice to those of the Water Framework Directive […] and the directives are not in conflict".

197 This is in line with the Directive on Port Reception Facilities, which in its Preamble (8th Recital) states that "Member States should be encouraged to take appropriate measures in accordance with Directive 2000/60/EC of the European Parliament and of the Council,

EU Member States are in the best position to determine the necessary measures in relation to their waters.[198]

According to the EU Commission, the existing scientific uncertainties and the expected increase in scrubbers in the course of the latest tightening of limit values in 2020 make it necessary to apply the precautionary principle.[199] Notwithstanding the fact that the legal consequences of the application of this principle cannot be determined in a general manner,[200] it may be necessary (particularly in highly sensitive waters such as seaports on inland waterways) to completely prohibit the discharge of scrubber washwater.[201] In any event, the EU Commission does not seem to see any reason to object to the restrictive practice of some EU Member States (including Germany), which have completely prohibited the discharge of scrubber washwater in parts of their inland and coastal waters in the implementation of the CDNI.[202] While State practice is inconsistent in this respect, there is almost unanimous agreement on the need to comply with the requirements of the WFD.[203]

### 2.3 *Relationship between Applicable International and EU Law*

With regard to the horizontal relationship between the relevant international agreements, on the one hand, and the vertical relationship between these agreements and the pertinent EU law instruments, on the other hand, the CDNI deserves particular attention due to the absolute prohibition of the discharge of scrubber washwater pursuant to its Article 3(1). In this respect, it should first be noted that the CDNI, as an autonomous international treaty, is binding only for the States Parties to it.[204] As the EU has not and could not accede to it, the CDNI is not part of the EU legal system. As the discharge

including discharge bans for wastewater from open loop scrubbers and certain cargo residues in their territorial waters".

198 EU Commission ENV.C.3/RH (n. 83), at 2.

199 Ibid.

200 EC Commission COM(2000) 1, of 2 February 2000, Application of the Precautionary Principle.

201 European Sustainable Shipping Forum 3rd Plenary Meeting, of 4 December 2014, Final Report Submission from the ESSF Sub-Groups, Annex 6, 1–2: "Recognize that because of local/regional surface water quality requirements which implement EU legislation such as the Water Framework Directive, the discharge from scrubber washwater in ports, estuaries and coastal waters to one nautical mile out to sea may be limited or even entirely prohibited even though that the washwater complies with the requirements in the IMO EGCS Guidelines".

202 Cf. EU Commission ENV.C.3/RH (n. 83), Annex I.

203 Ibid.

204 Cf. *Vienna Convention on the Law of Treaties*, adopted 23 May 1969, entered into force 27 January 1980, 1155 UNTS 331 [hereinafter VCLT], Art. 34.

prohibition prevents the transformation of SOx emissions into the air into scrubber washwater that is potentially harmful to the marine environment, the CDNI represents a particularly strict implementation of the prohibition of transformation of pollution.[205] In contrast, Regulation 4 of Annex VI to the MARPOL Convention allocates the decision whether exhaust gas cleaning systems (and the associated discharge of scrubber washwater, if any) are permissible to the Contracting States. For this reason, the CDNI cannot be regarded to conflict with the provisions of Annex VI to the MARPOL Convention on the discharge of scrubber washwater. States are free to submit themselves to stricter requirements provided for in other international treaties, and to not take a positive decision regarding the use of scrubbers under Regulation 4 of Annex VI to the MARPOL Convention. Nor should it be ignored that the issue of compatibility of the two regimes only arises to the extent to which the CDNI and the MARPOL Convention overlap in terms of their geographical scope, i.e., the inland waterways constituting internal waters including inland seaports. This is also the starting point of the IMO Guidelines for Exhaust Gas Cleaning Systems, which in para. 10.1.1 refer to the operation of scrubbers in ports and estuaries. Therefore, the MARPOL Convention and the CDNI are only applicable in parallel if and to the extent to which inland waterways – such as, for example, the Elbe or Rhine in Germany – are at least partially navigated by seagoing vessels.[206]

As regards the relevant EU law instruments, there is no apparent conflict between the CDNI and the MSFD or the WFD.[207] Quite the opposite, the absolute prohibition of discharges on which the regime of the CNDI is based is more in line with the objectives of both Directives than the prohibition subject to permission under Annex VI to the MARPOL Convention.

In contrast, a regime conflict between the CDNI on the one hand and the Sulphur Directive, on the other, cannot be excluded. This is due to the fact that unlike Regulation 4 of Annex VI to the MARPOL Convention, Article 8(1) of the Sulphur Directive does not leave the decision on the permissibility of operating exhaust gas cleaning systems and discharging scrubber washwater to the EU Member States. Rather, if and to the extent to which this provision is applicable in terms of its geographical scope, the operation of exhaust gas cleaning systems and the discharge of scrubber washwater *must* be permitted,

205 Inland waterways do not fall within the scope of UNCLOS or only to the extent that they are navigated by seagoing vessels, and Article 195 of UNCLOS is, therefore, not applicable within the full spatial scope of the CDNI.

206 Proelß and Schatz (n. 24), at 62.

207 Ibid.

provided that the remaining requirements of the Sulphur Directive are met. At the same time, it should be emphasized that the Sulphur Directive does not require maximum (or full) harmonization.[208] Pursuant to its Recital 14, the Sulphur Directive does "not prevent any Member State from maintaining or introducing more stringent protective measures in order to encourage early implementation with respect to the maximum sulphur content of marine fuels, for instance using emission abatement methods outside SOx Emission Control Areas". This is in line with Article 193 of the TFEU, stating that the "protective measures adopted pursuant to Article 192 shall not prevent any Member State from maintaining or introducing more stringent protective measures". Such measures "must be compatible with the Treaties" and "shall be notified to the Commission". On the field of environmental policy, the EU Member States are thus given the power to adopt more stringent protective measures provided that they are "compatible with the Treaties [and] notified to the Commission".[209] Against this background, the question arises whether the absolute prohibition of discharging scrubber washwater under the CNDI can be regarded as a more stringent protective measure within the meaning of Recital 14 of the Sulphur Directive and Article 193 of the TFEU.

In this respect, it is arguably not without relevance that the prohibition of discharges is codified in an international treaty. As far as can be seen, the CJEU has not yet decided whether a more stringent protective measure within the meaning of Article 193 of the TFEU can also be based on the conclusion of an international treaty. *Prima facie*, it seems that this question should be answered in the affirmative, as it does not seem to make a difference whether several EU Member States unilaterally adopt stricter protections in parallel, or whether they do so by way of concluding and implementing an international agreement. However, it should not be ignored that by concluding an international treaty such as the CDNI, legal obligations between the States Parties are established. The EU Member States could not easily be released from such treaty obligations even if it turns out at a later stage that the measures codified in the treaty are incompatible with EU law, and thus contrary to Article 193 of the TFEU.[210] In the specific case of the CDNI, the situation is further aggravated by the fact that Switzerland is not a Member State to the EU but party to the CDNI. At least in such situations, and based on the established case-law of the

208 Ibid.

209 Sulphur Directive, Preamble, 14th Recital.

210 Proelß and Schatz (n. 24), at 63.

CJEU, the risk of jeopardizing the autonomy of the EU legal order cannot be excluded.[211]

Furthermore, it must be taken into account that Article 193 of the TFEU is not applicable if an EU Member State decides to take action which is not covered by the substantive scope of the relevant norm of EU environmental law, which the Member State concerned intends to strengthen.[212] Article 193 of the TFEU only applies as far as the scope of the EU measure taken under Article 192 of the TFEU – the EU Sulphur Directive – extends.[213] In other words, EU Member States may only take *more stringent*, but not *different* protective measures on the basis of Article 193 of the TFEU.[214] In the present case, implementing an absolute ban on discharges of scrubber washwater is not a more stringent protective measure compared to the permission of alternative emission abatement methods, but a different measure which arguably does not fall within the scope of the Sulphur Directive, but within that of the WFD.[215] This can also be demonstrated by reference to the different objectives pursued by

211 Ibid. On the CJEU's broad understanding of autonomy, especially in connection with international treaty obligations of the EU Member States, see, e.g., A. Proelss, 'Dispute Settlement in Multi-Layered Constellations: International Law and the EU' (2014) 57 *German Yearbook of International Law* 225.

212 Proelß and Schatz (n. 24), at 63; Proelß and Schatz (n. 65), at 600. Cf. A. Käller, 'Art. 193 AEUV', in J. Schwarze, U. Becker, A. Hatje et al. (eds.), *EU-Kommentar* (*4th ed.*) (Nomos: Baden-Baden, 2019), [6].

213 M. Nettesheim, 'Art. 193 AEUV', in E. Grabitz, M. Hilf and M. Nettesheim (eds.), *Das Recht der Europäischen Union: EUV/AEUV* (*71th ed.*) (C. H. Beck: München, 2020), [7–8]; C. Callies, 'Art. 193 AEUV', in C. Callies and M. Ruffert (eds.), *EUV/AEUV: Das Verfassungsrecht der Europäischen Union mit Europäischer Grundrechtecharta: Kommentar* (*5th ed.*) (C. H. Beck: München, 2016), [5].

214 L. Krämer, 'Art. 193 AEUV', in H. von der Groeben, J. Schwarze and A. Hatje (eds.), *Europäisches Unionsrecht* (*7th ed.*) (Nomos: Baden-Baden, 2015), [7]; Käller (n. 212), at [6]; Nettesheim (n. 213), at [6–7]; Callies (n. 213), at [5].

215 See also the reference to the WFD (but not to the Sulphur Directive!) included in the Directive on Port Reception Facilities, Preamble, 8th Recital: "Member States should be encouraged to take appropriate measures in accordance with Directive 2000/60/EC of the European Parliament and of the Council, including discharge bans for wastewater from open loop scrubbers and certain cargo residues in their territorial waters". – The situation would be different, for example, if the EU had placed the use of scrubbers at the discretion of the EU Member States (as Annex VI to the MARPOL Convention does) and the States Parties to the CDNI had then completely banned them. Cf. also Judgment of the CJEU in Case C-232/97 *L. Nederhoff & Zn. v Dijkgraaf en hoogheemraden van het Hoogheemraadschap Rijnland* [51–61], on the question of the permissibility of adopting stricter conditions for granting authorizations concerning the discharge of substances into a body of water.

the Sulphur Directive on the one hand and the CDNI on the other:[216] While the Sulphur Directive, according to its Article 1(1), aims "to reduce the emissions of sulphur dioxide resulting from the combustion of certain types of liquid fuels and thereby to reduce the harmful effects of such emissions on man and the environment", the CDNI, according to its Preamble, concerns "the prevention and the collection, deposit and reception of waste with a view to its recycling and disposal in order to protect the environment and to ensure the safety and well-being of shipboard personnel and transport users". Moreover, Recital 15 of the Sulphur Directive contains a reference to Directive (EU) 2015/1535 Laying Down a Procedure for the Provision of Information in the Field of Technical Regulations and of Rules on Information Society Services.[217] Given that Articles 5(1) and 6(1) of Directive (EU) 2015/1535 oblige EU Member States to notify their draft technical regulations and provide for a standstill obligation of at least three months, this reference supports the view taken here.[218] This implies that the Sulphur Directive itself considers the possibility of *stricter* technical regulations, but not *different* measures such as discharge prohibitions as more stringent protective measures.[219]

It is true that if a domestic measure does not fall within the scope of Article 193 of the TFEU, this does not automatically imply that the measure concerned violates EU law. Indeed, in light of the shared competence of the EU and the EU Member States in the field of environmental policy,[220] the Member States may generally continue to adopt their own environmental legislation in fields not yet covered by EU environmental legislation.[221] In the present case, however, it should be borne in mind that the EU Member States are obliged to comply with the wording of the Sulphur Directive, which prescribes an obligation to permit alternative methods of emission reduction, including open

216 As regards the question whether an EU Member State measure constitutes a more stringent protective measure, the CJEU has consistently held that the objectives pursued by EU legislation are decisive. See, e.g., Judgment of the CJEU in Case C-6/03 *Deponiezweckverband Eiterköpfe v Land Rheinland-Pfalz* [36–41].

217 Directive (EU) 2015/1535 of the European Parliament and of the Council of 9 September 2015 Laying Down a Procedure for the Provision of Information in the Field of Technical Regulations and of Rules on Information Society Services OJ L 241/1.

218 On the previous Directive (EC) 98/34, the CJEU ruled that a breach of the notification and standstill obligation renders the national provision inapplicable. See Judgment of the CJEU in Case C-194/94 *CIA Security International SA v Signalson SA and Securitel SPRL* [49–50].

219 Proelß and Schatz (n. 24), at 64.

220 Cf. TFEU, Art. 4(2)(e).

221 Judgment of the CJEU in Cases C-379/08 and C-380/08 *ERG and others* [51]; Käller (n. 212), at [6].

loop scrubbers, if the remaining requirements of the Directive (which should, again, be interpreted in line with the WFD) are observed. The relevant issue here is thus completely covered by the pertinent EU environmental legislation, which is why it is not possible for the Member States to derogate from the provisions of the Sulphur Directive.

Against this background, if and to the extent to which a regime conflict cannot be avoided by way of interpreting Article 8(1) of the Sulphur Directive in line with the WFD,[222] the contradiction between the CDNI and the Sulphur Directive can only be resolved within the legal systems of EU Member States on the basis of the principle of primacy of EU law.[223] If and insofar as the two instruments overlap, the prohibition on discharges under the CDNI (and any national implementing legislation) must not be applied unless it complies with the Sulphur Directive.[224] At the level of international law, non-application of the prohibition of discharges under the CDNI indeed renders the EU Member States in violation of their treaty-obligations under the CDNI vis-à-vis the other States Parties. However, taking into account that with the exception of Switzerland, all States Parties to the CDNI are EU Member States, such a violation of international law could possibly be eliminated by way of amending or clarifying the CDNI.[225] In addition, it should also be kept in mind that Article 8(1) of the Sulphur Directive only applies to "ships of all flags" which are located in "ports, territorial seas, exclusive economic zones and pollution control zones". Therefore, the regime conflict, which must be resolved by reference to the principle of primacy of EU law, only arises in inland ports (which are specifically regulated by Article 8 of the Sulphur Directive),[226] taking into account that inland waterways are part of the "territory" of the Member States in terms of Article 5 of the Sulphur Directive, which only allows the operation of emission abatement methods "in closed mode". This results in the somewhat contradictory situation that a seagoing vessel travelling an inland waterway is prohibited by both the CDNI and Article 5 of the Sulphur Directive to discharge

222 See supra 2.2.5.

223 Cf. Judgment of the CJEU in Case C-6/64 *Costa v E.N.E.L.* 1270; M. Ruffert. 'Art. 1 AEUV', in Calliess and Ruffert (eds.) (n. 213), [16 et seq].

224 Proelß and Schatz (n. 24), at 64–65.

225 Ibid., at 65. An amendment of the CDNI and its Annexes can be done in accordance with Article 19 CDNI. In principle, according to Article 19(1) of the CDNI, any Contracting Party may submit a proposal for amendment to the Conference of the Parties. However, according to Article 19(3) of the CDNI, such amendments can only be adopted unanimously and, therefore, require the consent of Switzerland as the only Contracting Party that is not also an EU Member State.

226 There is nothing to suggest that Article 8 of the Sulphur Directive is only applicable to ports located at the coast, but not to inland ports called upon by seagoing vessels.

scrubber washwater, but may be allowed to do so on the basis of Article 8 of the Sulphur Directive once entering an inland port. The EU should therefore consider amending the Sulphur Directive so that it either leaves the decision of whether scrubber washwater discharges should be permitted to the Member States (allowing them to comply with the CDNI if they are parties to it) or to prohibit such discharges entirely. In contrast, scrubbers washing flue gas used in the inerting of cargo tanks of oil tankers do not fall within the scope of the Sulphur Directive and remain prohibited under the CDNI.

### 2.4 *Concluding Observations*

Under public international law, the management of scrubber washwater discharges is primarily regulated by Annex VI to the MARPOL Convention. While predominantly aiming at reducing pollution by ship exhaust gas at the source by limiting the SOx content of ship fuel, Regulation 4 of Annex VI to the MARPOL Convention allows for the use of alternative methods of reducing SOx emissions of vessels if such methods are at least as effective in terms of emissions reduction as the use of fuel with low sulphur content.

Exhaust gas cleaning systems are alternative reduction control methods, since they do not prevent the formation of pollutants as such, but can be used to remove pollutants from exhaust gas before they are released into the atmosphere. Pursuant to Regulation 4.1 of Annex VI to the MARPOL Convention, the decision to permit the use of such scrubbers as alternative SOx emission reduction methods is at the discretion of the Contracting Parties. Regulation 4 of Annex VI to the MARPOL Convention is further specified by the Guidelines for Exhaust Gas Cleaning Systems of the IMO, which were last updated in 2015. Even though these guidelines are not directly legally binding as such, they must be taken into account according to Regulation 4.1 of Annex VI to the MARPOL Convention. Para. 10 of the Guidelines contains requirements for the treatment of scrubber washwater. In particular, the Guidelines provide for continuous monitoring and recording of such washwater. Furthermore, they impose mandatory limit values for discharged washwater. Residues from scrubbers (so-called sludge) must be disposed of at appropriate land based reception facilities. Disposal of sludge at sea or incineration on board of ships is prohibited.

The CDNI aims to protect inland aquatic ecosystems that serve as waterways for shipping and to improve safety of navigation in such waterways by avoiding ship-related waste. According to Article 3(1) of the CDNI, the discharge of ship-generated waste by all ships, including seagoing vessels, is prohibited. Scrubber washwater can be classified as ship-generated waste. While such water is not expressly referred to by the CDNI, it must be considered as a form of "other waste generated from the operation of a vessel". In contrast to the situation under the international law of the sea in general and Annex VI to the MARPOL Convention in particular, the CDNI thus establishes an absolute prohibition for scrubber washwater discharges in inland waterways of the Contracting Parties.

At the level of EU law, the use of scrubbers is primarily regulated by the Sulphur Directive. This Directive serves to implement Annex VI to the MARPOL Convention on the level of EU law, and it equally provides for limits on permitted sulphur contents in marine fuels as the main instrument to reduce the SOx emissions. Similar to Annex VI to the MARPOL Convention, the Sulphur Directive also allows operation of alternative emission reduction methods. The Sulphur Directive essentially adopts the sulphur limits set out in Regulations 14.1 and 14.4 of Annex VI to the MARPOL Convention. However, in contrast to Annex VI to the MARPOL Convention, the Sulphur Directive does not leave the use of alternative emission reduction methods to the discretion of the Member States. Instead, Article 8(1) of the Sulphur Directive establishes a legal obligation of the Member States to permit in their domestic legislation the use of emission reduction methods that fulfill the conditions set out in the Sulphur Directive. In essence, these conditions implement the IMO Guidelines for Exhaust Gas Cleaning systems, but also add a few additional requirements.

Besides the Sulphur Directive, the Directive on Port Reception Facilities, the WFD and the MSFD are the main instruments applicable to scrubber washwater under EU law. The Directive on Port Reception Facilities has recently been revised in such a way that scrubber sludge and washwater are now covered by its terms. From the perspective of the MSFD, the discharge of scrubber washwater constitutes pollution. However, rather than imposing an absolute ban on pollution, the MSFD obliges EU Member States to implement the MSFD's objectives by way of developing marine strategies. The WFD, on the other hand, prohibits any deterioration in the status of surface waters. According to the CJEU, this prohibition obliges EU Member States, subject to the permissible granting of an exception, to refuse the authorization for a specific project if that project could lead to a deterioration in the status of a surface water body or jeopardize the timely achievement of a good surface water status.

As far as the relationship between the applicable EU legislation is concerned, the Sulphur Directive must be interpreted and implemented in such a way that it does not run counter to the general environmental protection objectives of the EU as codified, *inter alia*, in the MSFD and the WFD. Due to the absolute ban on the discharge of scrubber wastewater pursuant to Article 3(1) of the CDNI, the relationship of the CDNI with other relevant international and EU regulation raises questions of compatibility. This particularly applies to the relationship of the CDNI and the Sulphur Directive, as the latter does not leave the decision on the permissibility of the use of scrubbers as an alternative sulphur emission reduction method to the discretion of the EU Member States. Because of the different objectives of the CDNI and the Sulphur Directive, the ban on scrubber washwater discharges under the CDNI can arguably not be regarded as an admissible more stringent protective measure within the meaning of Article 193 of the TFEU. Consequently, the conflict between the CDNI and the Sulphur Directive within the legal system of EU Member States must, as far as the scope of the two instruments overlaps, be resolved by reference to the primacy of application of EU law. However, the CDNI and the Sulphur Directive only conflict in ports, provided that these ports are located in inland waterways accessed by seagoing vessels.

## 3 Discharges of Sewage

Ship-generated sewage, if discharged untreated into the sea, can cause health hazards, oxygen deficiency in the water and visible pollution in coastal areas.[227] The discharge of sewage by seagoing vessels into the sea and inland waters has thus been subject to detailed regulation by international and EU law. Different categories of sewage, namely "black water" and "grey water", have come to be accepted in legal practice. "Grey water" is defined by the IMO as "drainage from dishwater, galley sink, shower, laundry, bath and washbasin drains and does not include drainage from toilets, urinals, hospitals, and animal spaces, as defined in Regulation 1.3 of Annex IV to the MARPOL Convention and does not include drainage from cargo spaces".[228] In contrast, the term "black water" is not explicitly defined, but it is generally considered to correspond to the definition of "sewage" for the purposes of Annex IV to the MARPOL Convention, which essentially covers waste water from toilets, medical premises and spaces containing living animals, as well as other waste waters insofar as they are mixed with such drainages.[229] Notwithstanding these definitions, the classification and treatment of different types of ship-generated waste water ultimately depends on the applicable legal frameworks. Due to its particularly harmful effects, the following analysis focuses on sewage (i.e., "black water") as defined by Annex IV to the MARPOL Convention.

227 IMO, 'Prevention of Pollution by Sewage from Ships' 2020, at: <https://www.imo.org/en/OurWork/Environment/Pages/Sewage-Default.aspx> (accessed 17 November 2020).

228 IMO Marine Environment Protection Committee Resolution MEPC.227(64), of 5 October 2012, *Guidelines on Implementation of Effluent Standards and Performance Tests for Sewage Treatment Plants*, para. 2.7.

229 See infra 3.1.2.

## 3.1 *International Regulation of Sewage Discharges*

### 3.1.1 Part XII of UNCLOS

As ship-generated sewage undeniably constitutes "pollution" within the meaning of Article 1(1)(4) of UNCLOS,[230] the reduction and prevention of pollution from sewage falls within the scope of the anti-pollution provisions of UNCLOS, including Article 194(1) and Article 194(2) of UNCLOS. With respect to the discharge of sewage by ships, States Parties must implement the obligations contained in these provisions on the global level within the IMO (cf. Article 211(1) of UNCLOS) and also directly on the national level (cf. Article 211(2) of UNCLOS). On the global level, the issue of sewage discharges has been regulated within the framework of the MARPOL Convention.[231] On the regional level, relevant regulations have been included, for example, into the framework of the HELCOM Convention.[232]

### 3.1.2 Annex IV to the MARPOL Convention

The handling of sewage, including the issue of discharge, is addressed by Annex IV to the MARPOL Convention, which entered into force on 27 September 2003 (a revised version has been in force since 1 August 2005). Regulation 11 of Annex IV to the MARPOL Convention generally prohibits the discharge of sewage from ships into the sea. Article 2(3)(a) of the MARPOL Convention defines discharges (in relation to harmful substances or effluents containing such substances) as "any release howsoever caused from a ship" which "includes any escape, disposal, spilling, leaking, pumping, emitting or emptying".[233] "Sewage" within the meaning of Annex IV to the MARPOL Convention is defined as (1) "drainage and other wastes from any form of toilets and urinals",[234] (2) "drainage from medical premises (dispensary, sick bay, etc.) via wash basins, wash tubs and scuppers located in such premises",[235] (3) "drainage from spaces containing living animals",[236] and (4) "other waste waters when mixed with the [mentioned] drainages".[237] While grey water is

---

230 Cf. Bartenstein (n. 22), at [2]. On the definition of "pollution", cf. generally Y. Tanaka, 'Article 1', in Proelss (ed) (n. 20), 17, at [12–14].

231 See infra 3.1.2.

232 See infra 3.1.3.

233 For exceptions from the scope of the term "discharges", which are not, however, relevant here, see MARPOL Convention, Art. 2(3)(b).

234 MARPOL Convention, Annex IV, Regulation 1.3.1.

235 MARPOL Convention, Annex IV, Regulation 1.3.2.

236 MARPOL Convention, Annex IV, Regulation 1.3.3.

237 MARPOL Convention, Annex IV, Regulation 1.3.4.

thus not included in the scope of the relevant regulations,[238] if and to the extent that grey water on ships is not collected in separate holding tanks and therefore mixed with black water, the mixture is covered by Annex IV to the MARPOL Convention.

Several exceptions to the prohibition of sewage discharges are provided for in Regulation 11 of Annex IV to the MARPOL Convention. First, under Regulation 11.1.1, sewage which is not comminuted or disinfected may be discharged at a distance of not less than 12 nm from the "nearest land". The term "nearest land" refers to the baseline from which the territorial sea is measured.[239] The rule that the discharge of untreated sewage from ships is permitted at a certain distance from the coast is based on the idea that the oceans beyond the territorial sea (i.e., the high seas and, where claimed by the coastal State, the EEZ) are capable of receiving and degrading considerable quantities of sewage by natural bacterial activity. In 2006, the IMO adopted a recommendation on standards for discharge rates, which the competent authorities of the flag States should observe when determining discharge rates under their domestic law.[240] The requirements of Regulation 11.1.1 are somewhat more restrictive for sewage that has been stored in a holding tank[241] or originates from spaces containing living animals. Such sewage may not be discharged instantaneously but only at a moderate rate while the ship is moving and proceeding at not less than 4 knots. The rate of discharge must be approved by the competent authorities of the flag State (the "Administration")[242] based upon standards developed by the IMO (the "Organization").[243]

Second, Regulation 11.1.1 permits the discharge of comminuted and disinfected sewage at a distance of at least 3 nm from the nearest land if the sewage treatment system is approved by the competent authorities of the flag State in accordance with Regulation 9.1.2.

Third, Regulation 11.1.2 permits the discharge of sewage from sewage treatment plants without spatial restrictions provided that (1) the treatment plant

238 Cf. V. Schminke, *Die Einleitung häuslicher Schiffsabwässer nach nationalem und internationalem Recht* (Peter Lang: Frankfurt am Main, 2009), at 108–109.

239 Proelß and Schatz (n. 24), at 105. On the rules concerning baselines, see, e.g., D. R. Rothwell and T. Stephens, *The International Law of the Sea* 2nd edition (Hart Publishing: Oxford and Portland, 2016), at 33–53.

240 IMO Marine Environment Protection Committee Resolution MEPC.157(55), of 13 October 2006, *Recommendation on Standards for the Rate of Discharge of Untreated Sewage from Ships*, para. 3.

241 Pursuant to Regulation 1.4 of Annex IV to the MARPOL Convention, the term "[h]olding tank" refers to "a tank used for the collection and storage of sewage".

242 Cf. MARPOL Convention, Art. 2(5).

243 Cf. MARPOL Convention, Art. 2(7).

is approved by the IMO in accordance with Regulation 9.1.1 and (2) the test results of the treatment plant are recorded in the ship's International Sewage Pollution Prevention Certificate (ISPPC), and (3) the effluent must not "produce visible floating solids nor cause discoloration of the surrounding water".[244]

In addition, pursuant to Regulation 11.2, the discharge prohibition of Regulation 11.1 does not apply to ships operating only in waters under the jurisdiction of one State. Neither does it apply to visiting ships from other States while they are only in the waters of that State (the "host State") and are discharging sewage in accordance with the requirements imposed by that host State, which may be less stringent that Regulation 11.1.

Pursuant to Regulation 2.1 of Annex IV to the MARPOL Convention, Regulation 11.1 applies only to certain categories of ships "engaged in international voyages". Regulation 1.7 defines "international voyage" as "a voyage from a country to which the [MARPOL] Convention applies to a port outside such country, or conversely". As to the categories of ships to which the prohibition of sewage discharges applies, Annex IV to the MARPOL Convention distinguishes between "new ships" and "existing ships". Regulation 1.1.1 defines "new ships" as ships "for which the building contract is placed, or in the absence of a building contract, the keel of which is laid, or which is at a similar stage of construction, on or after the date of entry into force of [Annex IV to the MARPOL Convention]" (i.e., 27 September 2003). In the absence of a building contract, Regulation 1.1.2 defines "new ships" as ships "the delivery of which is three years or more after the date of entry into force of [Annex IV to the MARPOL Convention]". Conversely, "existing ships" are all ships which are not new ships.[245] Annex IV to the MARPOL Convention applies to new ships of 400 gross tonnage and upwards[246] and to new ships of less than 400 gross tonnage if they are certified to carry more than 15 persons.[247] As far as existing ships are concerned, the regulations of Annex IV to the MARPOL Convention apply under the same conditions, but only five years after their entry into force (27 September 2008).[248] Insofar as such existing ships are of a similar stage of construction before 2 October 1983, Regulation 2.2 requires the competent flag State authorities to ensure that such ships be equipped, "as far as practicable", to comply with Regulation 11. Annex IV to the MARPOL Convention is

244 Cf. IMO, *Guidelines on Implementation of Effluent Standards and Performance Tests for Sewage Treatment Plants* (n. 228).

245 MARPOL Convention, Annex IV, Regulation 1.2.

246 MARPOL Convention, Annex IV, Regulation 2.1.1.

247 MARPOL Convention, Annex IV, Regulation 2.1.2.

248 MARPOL Convention, Annex IV, Regulation 2.1.3 and 2.1.4.

not applicable to smaller seagoing ships, such as recreational craft, which do not fall into one of the categories of Regulation 1.1.

In the future, passenger ships will be subject to stricter requirements in special areas under Regulation 11.3 of Annex IV to the MARPOL Convention. These requirements are *leges speciales* in relation to the provisions of Regulation 11.1. Pursuant to Regulation 1.6 of Annex IV to the MARPOL Convention, "special areas" are sea areas where, for recognized technical reasons related to their oceanographical and ecological condition and the special character of their traffic, the adoption of special mandatory methods for the prevention of marine pollution by sewage is required. Pursuant to Regulation 1.6.1 of Annex IV to the MARPOL Convention, the only special area which has so far been designated is the Baltic Sea area as defined in Regulation 1.11.2 of Annex I to the MARPOL Convention.[249]

Regulation 1.10 of Annex IV to the MARPOL Convention defines passenger ships as ships carrying more than 12 passengers.[250] The reason why these ships are subject to stricter standards in the Baltic Sea is that the Baltic Sea, due to its natural features, has a slow water exchange with the North Sea and is therefore particularly vulnerable to increased nutrient inputs (including from black water).[251] According to the revised[252] Regulation 11.3 of Annex IV to the MARPOL Convention, the discharge of sewage within the special area is prohibited (1) for new passenger ships[253] as from 1 June 2019, (2) for existing passenger ships as from 1 June 2019, (3) for new passenger ships as from 1 June 2019 and (4) for existing passenger ships operating on a direct route to

249 IMO, 'Prevention of Pollution by Sewage from Ships' (n. 227).

250 Under Regulation 1.9 of Annex IV to the MARPOL Convention, a passenger is defined as any person other than (1) the master and members of the crew or other persons employed or engaged in any capacity on board a ship on the business of that ship and (2) children under one year of age. Persons are, in accordance with Regulation 1.8, crew members and passengers.

251 On the problem of eutrophication of the Baltic Sea and the legality of sea-based engineering measures as a remedy, see H. Ringbom, B. Bohman and S. Ilvessalo, *Combatting Eutrophication in the Baltic Sea: Legal Aspects of Sea-Based Engineering Measures* (Brill: Leiden, 2018).

252 IMO Marine Environment Protection Committee Resolution MEPC.275(69), of 22 April 2016, *Establishment of the Date on Which Regulation 11.3 of MARPOL Annex IV in Respect of the Baltic Sea Special Area Shall Take Effect.*

253 Pursuant to Regulation 1.10 of Annex IV to the MARPOL Convention, new passenger ships, as defined in Regulation 11.3.a of Annex IV to the MARPOL Convention, are passenger ships (1) for which the building contract was awarded on or after 1 January 2016 or, in the absence of a building contract, the keel of which was laid or which were at a similar stage of construction on that date, or (2) which were delivered at least two years after 1 January 2016.

or from a port located outside the special area or on a direct route from a port located east of longitude 28°10′ East within the special area without a further stopover in another port, from 1 June 2023.

The prohibition in Regulation 11.3 has entered into force for new but not yet for existing passenger ships. Pursuant to Regulation 11.3 in conjunction with Regulation 13.2 of Annex IV to the MARPOL Convention, the IMO may also determine later dates for the entry into force of the discharge prohibition. Ultimately, it will depend on when the Contracting Parties have established a sufficient number of port reception facilities in the region of the special area, in accordance with Regulation 13.1, in order to ensure the practicability of the prohibition of sewage discharges. However, States bordering the Baltic Sea have already informed the IMO that sufficient port reception facilities are now available.[254]

An exception to the prohibition in Regulation 11.3 is made for discharges from passenger ships if (1) they operate an approved sewage treatment plant, (2) they have been certified by the Administration as complying with the operational requirements of Regulation 9.2.1, and (3) the effluent does not produce visible floating solids and does not cause discoloration of the surrounding water. Regulation 13.2 of Annex IV to the MARPOL Convention clarifies that until the prohibition in Regulation 11.3 comes into force, the general prohibition of discharge in Regulation 11.1 applies.

Regulation 3 of Annex IV to the MARPOL Convention provides that the prohibitions of Regulations 11.1 and 11.3 do not apply to the discharge of sewage where such discharge is necessary for the safety of a ship and persons on board and for the purpose of saving life at sea. A further exception is made when the discharge is caused by damage to a ship or its equipment and all reasonable precautions have been taken both before and after the damage to prevent and minimize the discharge.[255]

In order to prevent circumvention of the provisions of the other Annexes to the MARPOL Convention, Regulation 11.4 of Annex IV to the MARPOL Convention stipulates that in the case of mixing of sewage with waste or waste water within the meaning of the other Annexes to the MARPOL Convention, the provisions of the other Annexes must be complied with.

Regulation 12.1 of Annex IV to the MARPOL Convention obliges all Contracting Parties that require ships operating in waters under their

---

254 See HELCOM Maritime, 'Baltic Sea Sewage Port Reception Facilities' (2018), at: <https://helcom.fi/media/publications/HELCOM-Sewage-PRF-Overview_Baltic-Sea_2018_August_2018.pdf> (accessed 17 November 2020).

255 MARPOL Convention, Annex IV, Regulation 3.2.

jurisdiction and visiting ships (while in their waters) to comply with the discharge conditions of Regulation 11.1 to provide facilities for the reception of sewage without causing undue delay to the ships and sufficient to meet the requirements of the ships using them. The obligation to provide port reception facilities under regulation 12.1 of Annex IV to the MARPOL Convention thus serves to ensure the existence of the infrastructure necessary to comply with the prohibitions on sewage discharges.

#### 3.1.3 HELCOM Convention

The 1992 Convention on the Protection of the Marine Environment of the Baltic Sea Area (HELCOM Convention),[256] which entered into force on 17 January 2000, aims to protect the Baltic Sea against all forms of deterioration and to maintain and restore its ecological balance.[257] The scope of the HELCOM Convention covers the "Baltic Sea Area" which, according to Article 1 of the HELCOM Convention, includes "the Baltic Sea and the entrance to the Baltic Sea bounded by the parallel of the Skaw in the Skagerrak at 57° 44.43′N"". The HELCOM Convention is explicitly applicable to the internal waters, whose landward limits may be designated by the Contracting Parties.[258]

Pursuant to Article 5 of the HELCOM Convention, all Contracting Parties are under a duty to "undertake to prevent and eliminate pollution of the marine environment of the Baltic Sea Area caused by harmful substances from all sources" (according to the provisions of the HELCOM Convention) and to implement the procedures and measures listed in Annex I to the HELCOM Convention to this end. Article 8(1) of the HELCOM Convention obliges the Contracting Parties to take the measures described in Annex IV to the HELCOM Convention to protect the Baltic Sea Area from pollution by ships. In addition, Article 8(2) of the HELCOM Convention requires the Contracting Parties to develop and implement uniform requirements for the establishment of facilities for the reception of ship-generated wastes, taking into account, *inter alia*, the special needs of passenger ships in the Baltic Sea Area.

The provisions of Annex IV to the HELCOM Convention concerning the discharge of sewage are closely aligned with the corresponding provisions of Annex IV to the MARPOL Convention.[259] Pursuant to Regulation 3(2)(a) of

256 *Convention on the Protection of the Marine Environment of the Baltic Sea*, adopted 9 April 1992, entered into force 3 May 1980, 2099 UNTS 195.

257 Cf. HELCOM Convention, Art. 3(1).

258 HELCOM Convention, Art. 1 defines internal waters as the "waters on the landward side of the base lines from which the breadth of the territorial sea is measured up to the landward limit according to the designation by the Contracting Parties".

259 For further details, see, e.g., Schminke (n. 238), at 112, with further references.

Annex IV to the HELCOM Convention, discharges in relation to harmful substances or effluents containing such substances are defined (in line with Annex IV to the MARPOL Convention)[260] as "any release howsoever caused from a ship" and include "any escape, disposal, spilling, leaking, pumping, emitting or emptying". Regulation 4(1) and (3) of Annex IV to the HELCOM Convention render Annex IV to the MARPOL Convention applicable, thereby incorporating the rules concerning sewage discharges. In particular, Regulation 4(3)(a) of Annex IV to the HELCOM Convention requires the Contracting Parties to apply the provisions on the discharge of sewage in Regulations 11.1 and 11.3 of Annex IV to the MARPOL Convention. It follows that the provisions of Annex IV to the HELCOM Convention equally apply only to black water, not to grey water.[261] Similarly, under Regulation 4(3)(b) of Annex IV to the HELCOM Convention, the Contracting Parties are obliged to provide reception facilities for sewage in ports or at offshore terminals in accordance with Regulation 12.1 of Annex IV to the MARPOL Convention.

However, Annex IV to the HELCOM Convention also contains provisions going *beyond* Annex IV to the MARPOL Convention.[262] Pursuant to Regulation 5(A) of Annex IV to the HELCOM Convention, all other ships equipped with toilets, including recreational craft, must comply with the discharge provisions of Regulations 11.1 and 11.3 of Annex IV to the MARPOL Convention. These types of ships are not covered by the categories of ships listed in Regulation 2 of Annex IV to the MARPOL Convention. In addition, Regulation 5(B) of Annex IV to the HELCOM Convention requires these ships to be equipped with a toilet retention system in accordance with the guidelines approved by the Helsinki Commission.[263] Regulation 5(C)(1) of Annex IV to the HELCOM Convention prescribes that Regulation 12.1 of Annex IV to the MARPOL Convention applies "as appropriate" to ships referred to in Regulation 5(A), which in turn means that Contracting Parties must provide adequate port reception facilities. Under Regulation 5(D) of Annex IV to the HELCOM Convention, Contracting Parties may make use of a variety of exceptions from the abovementioned rules in respect of certain types of pleasure craft and other ships fitted with toilets and not referred to in Regulation 2 of Annex IV to the MARPOL Convention. However, these exceptions require

260 Cf. also the limitations of the concept of "discharges" in HELCOM Convention, Annex IV, Regulation 3(2)(b).

261 Cf. Proelß and Schatz (n. 24), at 109.

262 Schminke (n. 238), at 113; Proelß and Schatz (n. 24), at 109.

263 HELCOM Recommendation 22/1, of 21 March 2001, *Installation of Toilet Retention Systems and Standard Connections for the Sewage on Board Existing Fishing Vessels, Working Vessels and Pleasure Craft.*

that (1) the installation of toilet retention systems in these pleasure craft and other ships is technically difficult or the costs of installation is high compared to the value of the ship (according to guidelines approved by the Helsinki Commission) and (2) that these pleasure craft and other ships were built before 1 January 2000.

### 3.1.4 CDNI

The CDNI contains regulations concerning the discharge of sewage from ships. These regulations apply to all inland waterways used for general traffic.[264] According to Article 1(e) of the CDNI, domestic waste water is included in the definition of "[o]ther waste generated from the operation of the vessel" as defined in Annex 2 Part C to the CDNI. According to Art. 8.01(a) Annex 2 Part C Chapter VIII to the CDNI, domestic waste water is "wastewater from galleys, dining rooms, washing facilities and laundry facilities, and water containing faecal matter". In contrast to Annex IV to the MARPOL Convention, the CDNI thus covers both black water and grey water.

Article 9.01(3) of Annex 2 Part C Chapter IX to the CDNI prohibits the discharge of domestic waste water for only two categories of ships. Pursuant to Article 9.01(3)(a) of Annex 2 Part C Chapter IX to the CDNI, this prohibition has applied to cruise vessels with more than 50 sleeping berths since 1 May 2005. In addition, pursuant to Article 9.01(3)(a) of Annex 2 Part C Chapter IX to the CDNI, it has applied to passenger vessels authorized to carry more than 50 passengers since 1 January 2010. According to Article 9.03(4) of Annex 2 Part C Chapter IX to the CDNI, ship masters whose ships are subject to the prohibition of domestic waste water discharges must ensure that such sewage is collected in an appropriate manner on board the vessel and deposited at a reception station or facility in accordance with Article 8.02(3) of Annex 2 Part C Chapter VIII to the CDNI, unless the passenger ship is equipped with an on-board sewage treatment plant in accordance with Article 9.01(4) of Annex 2 Part C Chapter IX to the CDNI. If a passenger ship has an approved on-board sewage treatment plant which complies with the limit and control values laid down in Annex V to the CDNI, it is exempted from the prohibition of discharge in accordance with Article 9.01(4) of Annex 2 Part C Chapter IX to the CDNI.

Discharges from ships which do not fall into one of the two mentioned categories are expressly permitted under Article 9.01(3) of Appendix 2 Part C Chapter IX to the CDNI. Consequently, the most important ships operating in inland waterways, namely, motorized freight vessels, are not affected by the

---

264 See supra 2.1.3.

prohibition of domestic waste water discharges.[265] In addition, Article 9.02 of Annex 2 Part C Chapter IX to the CDNI allows States Parties to agree on an appropriate procedure for exemptions and to specify the conditions under which such exemptions can be considered equivalent for ships to which the discharge prohibition of Article 9.01(3) of Annex 2 Part C Chapter IX to the CDNI applies, but for which compliance with the discharge prohibition is "difficult to achieve in practice or would incur unreasonable expense". Such a decision was taken by resolution in 2013.[266] The annex to this resolution provides that on passenger ships with on-board sewage treatment systems which were installed for operation outside the scope of the CDNI (1) before 1 November 2009, (2) after 31 October 2009 but before 1 January 2011, or (3) before 1 January 2011, these systems may continue to operate under certain conditions, provided certain requirements are met.[267]

In the present context, it should be noted that Article 9.01(5) of Annex II Part C Chapter IX to the CDNI exempts seagoing vessels in seaports located on maritime navigation routes from the prohibition of discharge. However, this exemption is granted only on the condition that these vessels are subject to the provisions of the MARPOL Convention (because seaports located on maritime navigation routes constitute internal waters in which the MARPOL Convention applies), which means that the provisions of Annex IV to the MARPOL Convention concerning sewage discharges are applicable.[268]

## 3.2 *EU Legislation concerning the Discharge of Sewage*

### 3.2.1 MSFD, WFD and Directive on Port Reception Facilities

With regard to the requirements of the MSFD and the WFD, reference can be made to sections 2.2.3. and 2.2.4. above. Recital 3 of the Directive on Port Reception Facilities[269] makes it clear that the Directive, *inter alia*, serves to implement the MARPOL Convention and, in particular, the obligation to provide adequate reception facilities for waste water in ports, as laid down in the MARPOL Convention.[270] For sewage, this obligation arises from Regulation 12.1 of Annex IV to the MARPOL Convention. The Directive on Port Reception Facilities applies to "waste from ships", which according to Article 2(3) includes

265 Reimann (n. 78), at 57–58.
266 CDNI Res. CDNI 2013-II-5, of 12 December 2013, *Dispositions Dérogatoires Pour Difficultés Insurmontables Conformément à l'Article 9.02 de l'Annexe 2 Pour Les Stations d'Épuration de Bord.*
267 Ibid.
268 Proelß and Schatz (n. 24), at 111.
269 Cf. supra 2.2.2.
270 Cf. Schminke (n. 238), at 124, with further details.

"all waste [...] which is generated during the service of a ship or during loading, unloading and cleaning operations and which falls within the scope of Annexes I, II, IV, V and VI to MARPOL Convention". In light of the express reference to Annex IV to the MARPOL Convention, it only covers black water and grey water mixed with black water to the extent defined there, but not grey water.[271]

### 3.2.2 Relationship between Applicable EU Directives

With regard to the question of the permissibility of sewage discharges, the relevant EU Directives are in harmony. In particular, the strict requirements of the Directive on Port Reception Facilities support the implementation of the requirements of the WFD insofar as the former Directive's scope is concerned (i.e., with regard to black water).[272] Conversely, the fact that the Directive on Port Reception Facilities lacks provisions regulating grey water does not necessarily lead to the conclusion that the discharge of grey water is permitted, particularly as such discharges could conflict with the requirements of the WFD.[273]

## 3.3 *Relationship between Applicable International Law and EU Law*

With regard to the relationship between the relevant provisions of the applicable international legal instruments (UNCLOS, MARPOL Convention, HELCOM Convention, and CDNI), the only conflicts that can be discerned relate to seagoing vessels operating on *inland* maritime waterways (i.e., rivers leading up to seaports located inland).

First, the MARPOL Convention serves to implement the provisions on marine environmental protection laid down in Part XII of UNCLOS. Second, Annex IV to the HELCOM Convention incorporates the relevant provisions of Annex IV to the MARPOL Convention for the discharge of sewage and extends the scope of these provisions to additional categories of ships. Third, the CDNI's prohibition of domestic waste water discharges is explicitly not applicable to seagoing ships in seaports located on maritime navigation routes to the extent that these ships are covered by the MARPOL Convention. In this respect, however, it is unclear whether the extension of the relevant provisions of Annex IV to the MARPOL Convention to all other ships, including recreational craft if they are fitted with toilets (as provided by Regulation 5(A) of Annex IV to the HELCOM Convention), foreseen by the HELCOM Convention also falls within the scope

271 Ibid., at 132, 142.

272 Proelß and Schatz (n. 24), at 112.

273 Ibid. Contra: Schminke (n. 238), at 141–145.

of the exception in Article 9.01(5) of Annex 2 Part C Chapter IX to the CDNI. This provision does not expressly refer to the HELCOM Convention. However, since the effect of Regulation 5(A) of Annex IV to the HELCOM Convention is that Regulations 11.1 and 11.3 of Annex IV to the MARPOL Convention are also applicable to the ships referred to in the pertinent standard, a harmonizing interpretation suggests that these ships "are subject" to the relevant provisions of Annex IV to the MARPOL Convention for States Parties of the CDNI that are simultaneously States Parties to the MARPOL Convention and the HELCOM Convention.[274]

However, in view of the clear wording of Article 9.01(5) of Annex 2 Part C Chapter IX to the CDNI, seagoing vessels located on maritime navigation routes (and not in the seaports on such routes) are *not* covered. For seagoing vessels in these areas, the prohibition of domestic waste water discharges in Article 9.01(3) of Annex 2 Part C Chapter VIII to the CDNI therefore remains applicable in addition to the requirements of Annex IV to the MARPOL Convention. It follows that discharges of domestic waste water from ships other than those mentioned in Article 9.01(3) of Annex 2 Part C Chapter IX to the CDNI are expressly permitted pursuant to the second sentence of that provision. This, however, conflicts with the extension of the scope of application of Regulations 11.1 and 11.3 of Annex IV to the MARPOL Convention to "all other ships" by Regulation 5(A) of Annex IV to the HELCOM Convention. This conflict of norms can be resolved by reference to the *lex specialis* principle.[275] While the CDNI could be considered as the more specific treaty from a geographical point of view, the provisions of Article 6(1) of the CNDI, Article 2.03(3) of Annex 2 Part A Chapter II to the CDNI, Article 5.03 of Annex 2 Part B Chapter V to the CDNI, and Article 9.01(5) of Annex 2 Part C Chapter IX to the CDNI demonstrate that this Convention does not exhaustively regulate the matter of domestic waste water discharges for seagoing ships, but rather accepts the MARPOL Convention as the more specific regulatory instrument in this regard. For this reason, the requirements of Regulations 11.1 and 11.3 of Annex IV to the MARPOL Convention must also be applied with regard to seagoing vessels located on inland maritime navigation routes.

As far as the relationship between the relevant international treaties and EU legislation is concerned, it cannot be excluded that discharges of harmful sewage that are not prohibited by the MARPOL Convention, the HELCOM Convention or the CDNI could nevertheless be prohibited under the WFD. In these situations, however, there is no direct regime conflict, taking into account

274 Proelß and Schatz (n. 24), at 112.

275 Ibid., at 113.

that the applicable international legal regulations only *exempt* discharges from prohibitions, but – with the exception of the CDNI – do not explicitly *permit* them. Even to the extent that discharges from ships are expressly permitted under Article 9.01(3) of Annex 2 Part C Chapter IX to the CDNI, this does not automatically collide with the prohibition of deterioration under Article 4(1)(a)(i) of the WFD. It must be recalled that this prohibition does not apply to every significant impairment of a body of water. Rather, Article 4(1)(a)(i) of the WFD is only activated if the status of at least one of the "quality elements" in Annex V of the WFD deteriorates by one class as a result of the specific discharge in question. Therefore, a violation of the prohibition of deterioration under the WFD may only be determined on a case-by-case basis and in exceptional situations.[276] Whenever such a regime conflict arises, however, the permission of discharges in Article 9.01(3) of Annex 2 Part C Chapter VIII to the CDNI must be disregarded vis-à-vis the WFD in view of the primacy of EU law.

Finally, no conflict exists between the applicable international law rules and the Directive on Port Reception Facilities. This Directive explicitly serves the implementation of Regulation 12.1 of Annex IV to the MARPOL Convention, which obliges Contracting Parties to provide port reception facilities that enable vessels to comply with the prohibition of sewage discharges under Regulations 11.1 and 11.3 of Annex IV to the MARPOL Convention. Therefore, there is no reason to interpret the Directive's provisions as imposing an absolute prohibition on sewage discharges even for discharges permitted under Regulations 11.1 and 11.3 of Annex IV to the MARPOL Convention.[277] Article 7(1) of the Directive on Port Reception Facilities contains an obligation of masters of ships to deliver all waste carried on board *before departure*. This obligation concerns conduct *in port* and does not regulate the issue of whether discharges are permissible *during the voyage* to the port under Regulation 11.1 of Annex IV to the MARPOL Convention.[278] Admittedly, according to the clear wording of Article 7(1) of the Directive on Port Reception Facilities, even sewage that may be discharged into the sea under Regulations 11.1 and 11.3 of Annex IV to the MARPOL Convention must be discharged before leaving port. This does not mean, however, that the obligation to dispose of sewage also implies a prohibition on discharges on the way to a port.

---

276 Ibid.

277 Ibid. Contra: Schminke (n. 238), at 135.

278 Proelß and Schatz (n. 24), at 113.

## 3.4 *Concluding Observations*

On the global level, the discharge of sewage from seagoing ships is regulated by Annex IV to the MARPOL Convention. The relevant provisions cover the discharge of black water, but not that of grey water. In accordance with Regulation 11 of Annex IV to the MARPOL Convention, the discharge of sewage is prohibited unless one of the explicit exceptions applies. This prohibition is complemented by an obligation of the Contracting Parties to establish port reception facilities for sewage. In the Baltic Sea region, the MARPOL Convention is complemented by the requirements of Annex IV to the HELCOM Convention, which goes – to some extent – beyond those of Annex IV to the MARPOL Convention. For example, Annex IV to the HELCOM Convention prescribes that in addition to the categories of ships mentioned in Annex IV to the MARPOL Convention, all other types of ships (including, in particular, pleasure craft) must comply with the discharge requirements of Annex IV to the MARPOL Convention if the ships concerned are fitted with toilets. Furthermore, these ships have to be fitted with a toilet retention system that complies with the applicable guidelines approved by the Helsinki Commission.

Under the CDNI, domestic waste water is classified as "other waste generated from the operation of the vessel" within the meaning of Annex 2 Part C to the CDNI. Unlike the MARPOL Convention and the HELCOM Convention, the CNDI defines domestic waste water as covering both black and grey water. The CDNI only prohibits the discharge of sewage for two categories of ships: First, for cruise vessels with more than 50 sleeping berths. Second, for passenger ships permitted to carry more than 50 passengers. Domestic waste water must be collected in an appropriate manner and discharged at a reception facility unless the ship is equipped with an onboard sewage treatment plant. If a ship is equipped with such a system that complies with the requirements of Annex V to the CDNI, it is exempted from the prohibition of sewage discharge. Discharges from ships not falling into one of the two aforementioned categories are expressly permitted. Hence, those ships which have the largest environmental impact on inland waterways, namely freighters, are not subject to the prohibition of the discharge of sewage.

On inland maritime waterways, a conflict between the CDNI and Annex IV to the HELCOM Convention exists insofar as the former explicitly permits discharges of domestic waste water from ships other than those mentioned in Article 9.01(3) of Annex 2 Part C Chapter IX to the CDNI. The reason for this conflict is that Regulation 5(A) of Annex IV to the HELCOM Convention extends the scope of application of Regulations 11.1 and 11.3 of Annex IV to the MARPOL Convention to "all other ships", thus also to ships covered by the CDNI's explicit permission of discharges. This conflict must be resolved in favour of the prohibition of discharges in Annex IV of the HELCOM Convention through the application of the *lex specialis* principle. On the level of EU law, the requirements of the MSFD and the WFD have to be respected insofar as they apply to the discharge of sewage. Furthermore, according to the Directive on Port Reception Facilities, black water must generally be disposed in port reception facilities of the next port of call. However, this does not apply if the ship has sufficient storage capacity for all ship-generated sewage that has been accumulated and will be accumulated during the intended voyage of the ship until the port of delivery, and provided that the port of delivery has adequate port reception facilities.

## 4 Discharges of Ballast Water

Ballast water serves to regulate the trim, heeling, draught, stability or tension of a ship.[279] For this purpose, ballast water is taken on board the ship and discharged as required – which may happen at different locations around the world.[280] In situations where ballast water that has been taken up at one location contains species alien at the other location, a significant risk exists that harmful alien species are being introduced into marine ecosystems at the location where it is discharged.[281] To reduce this environmental risk, which is recognized by Article 196(1) of UNCLOS, binding regulation for the discharge of ballast water and the disposal of sediments from ballast tanks has been developed at the international level – predominantly under the auspices of the IMO.

### 4.1 *International Regulation of Ballast Water Discharges*

#### 4.1.1 Obligation to Combat the Introduction of Harmful Alien Species

The threat to the marine environment posed by the introduction of invasive alien species is recognized by Part XII of UNCLOS. At the outset, it must be noted that the scope of the general obligation codified in Article 192 of UNCLOS it not restricted to the prevention, reduction or control of pollution, i.e., the introduction of substances or energy into the sea. Therefore, Article 192 of UNCLOS may be considered broad enough to also embrace the obligation to protect and preserve the marine environment in the face of risks caused by the introduction of alien species with respect to the state of marine ecosystems.[282] This is not without relevance, taking into account that it is not completely

279 IMO (n. 10).
280 Ibid.
281 Ibid.
282 Cf. Czybulka (n. 20), at [3]; Czybulka (n. 44), at [9].

clear whether the introduction of alien species constitutes "pollution of the marine environment" within the meaning of Article 1(1)(4) of UNCLOS, which would render the anti-pollution provisions of Part XII of UNCLOS, and particularly Article 194, applicable.[283] That said, there are good reasons to argue that while the organisms in ballast water themselves are not actually "substances" within the meaning of Article 1(1)(4) of UNCLOS, the ballast water containing such organisms is indeed a "substance",[284] which is why the discharge of ballast water and sediments as such constitutes pollution.[285]

In any event, Article 196(1) of UNCLOS (more precisely, the second part of that provision)[286] contains a special obligation of the States Parties to "take all measures necessary to prevent, reduce and control [...] the intentional or accidental introduction of species, alien or new, to a particular part of the marine environment, which may cause significant and harmful changes thereto". This obligation is designed as an obligation of due diligence ("take all measures necessary to prevent, reduce and control"), meaning that it requires States Parties to enact and enforce suitable legislation within the limits of its prescriptive and enforcement jurisdiction.[287] While Article 196(1) of UNCLOS distinguishes between "alien" and "new" species, only "alien species" are of particular relevance in the context of ballast water management.[288] This term is not defined in UNCLOS, but according to a common (non-binding) definition, an alien species is

> species, subspecies, or lower taxon occurring outside of its natural range (past or present) and dispersal potential (i.e. outside the range it occupies naturally or could not occupy without direct or indirect introduction or care by humans) and includes any part, gametes or propagule of such species that might survive and subsequently reproduce.[289]

---

283 Czybulka (n. 44), at [20].

284 Bartenstein (n. 22), at [2].

285 R. Zink, *Das Ballastwasser-Übereinkommen der internationalen Seeschifffahrts-Organisation von 2004: Anwendung in Nord- und Ostsee* (Nomos: Baden-Baden, 2016), at 128–148.

286 M. H. Nordquist, N. R. Grandy, S. Rosenne et al. (eds.), *United Nations Convention on the Law of the Sea 1982: A Commentary*, Vol. 4 (Martinus Nijhoff: Dordrecht, 1991), at 73–76; Czybulka (n. 44), at [1].

287 Cf. *Request for an Advisory Opinion Submitted by the Sub-Regional Fisheries Commission (SRFC)* (n. 21), at [120].

288 "New species", on the other hand, refers to new breeds and species modified by biotechnology. See Czybulka (n. 44), at [14].

289 IUCN, 'Guidelines for the Prevention of Biodiversity Loss Caused by Alien Invasive Species' (2000), <http://www.issg.org/pdf/guidelines_iucn.pdf> (accessed 17 November 2020), para. 3. Cf. Czybulka (n. 44), at [14].

In order to determine whether an alien species is an invasive species that is harmful to the marine environment, recourse may be made to Article 8(h) of the Convention on Biological Diversity,[290] which contains an obligation to "[p]revent the introduction of, control or eradicate those alien species which threaten ecosystems, habitats or species".[291] The applicability of Article 196(1) of UNCLOS does not depend on whether harmful alien species are introduced intentionally or unintentionally.[292] In fact, the introduction of alien species through the discharge of ballast water is usually done unintentionally.[293]

The ballast water problem can be addressed on the basis of Article 196(1) in conjunction with Article 197 of UNCLOS at the global and regional levels, which – as shown below – has been done under the auspices of the IMO.[294]

### 4.1.2 International Convention for the Control and Management of Ships' Ballast Water and Sediments

#### 4.1.2.1 *Objectives and Scope*

The BWM Convention[295] aims to protect marine ecosystems by preventing, minimizing and eventually eliminating the transfer of harmful aquatic organisms and pathogens through the control and management of ships' ballast water and sediments.[296] Therefore, the BWM Convention serves to implement the obligation under Article 196(1) of UNCLOS insofar as the risks of ballast water and sediments are concerned.[297] As of 2 March 2021, the BWM

---

290 *Convention on Biological Diversity*, adopted 5 June 1992, entered into force 29 December 1993, 1760 UNTS 79.

291 Czybulka (n. 44), at [14]; Proelß and Schatz (n. 24), at 85. Cf. also, more generally with respect to using the CBD as interpretive guidance in the context of UNCLOS, *South China Sea Arbitration* (n. 19), at [945].

292 Czybulka (n. 44), at [15]; Zink (n. 285), at 152.

293 Czybulka (n. 44), at [15].

294 Zink (n. 285), at 153–154; M. S. Karim, *Prevention of Pollution of the Marine Environment from Vessels: The Potential and Limits of the International Maritime Organisation* (Springer: New York, 2015), at 67–83.

295 BWM Convention (n. 9).

296 Cf. BWM Convention, Preamble and Art. 2(1). On the BWM Convention, see generally M. Tsimplis, 'Alien Species Stay Home: The International Convention for the Management of Ships' Ballast Water and Sediments 2004' (2005) 19 *International Journal of Marine and Coastal Law* 411; M. H. Fonseva de Souza Rolim, *The International Law on Ballast Water: Preventing Biopollution* (Martinus Nijhoff Publishers: Leiden/Boston, 2008), at 97–144; A. Zink, 'The IMO's Ballast Water Management Convention of 2004: A Decade of Evolution and Challenges' (2015) 29 *Ocean Yearbook* 441.

297 Cf. BWM Convention, Preamble, 1st Recital. See also N. Windemuth, *Meeresverschmutzung durch den internationalen Seeverkehr: Ausweitung staatlicher Kontroll- und Interventionsrechte zum Schutz der Meeresumwelt* (Peter Lang: Frankfurt am Main, 2011), at 251;

Convention had 86 Contracting States, the combined merchant fleets of which were estimated by the IMO to "constitute approximately 91.12% of the gross tonnage of the world's merchant fleet".[298]

As the detailed and rather technical BWM Convention regime cannot be presented here in its entirety, this analysis is restricted to the essential rules concerning the BWM Convention's scope as well as the discharge of ballast water and sediments from ballast tanks.

The BWM Convention applies to ships entitled to fly the flag of its States Parties[299] and to ships that, while not being entitled to fly the flag of a State Party, "operate under the authority of a Party".[300] The term "authority" refers to jurisdiction to impose environmental standards on ships, which includes the port State's jurisdiction with respect to the protection of the marine environment in its internal waters.[301] In the case of vessels of States that are not States Parties to the BWM Convention, Article 3(3) of the BWM Convention obliges the States Parties to apply the provisions of the BWM Convention to the extent necessary to ensure that such vessels do not receive more favourable treatment than vessels of States Parties.[302] The purpose of this provision is to prevent non-party vessels from obtaining a competitive advantage over vessels of States Parties by benefiting from lower costs and faster handling in ports.[303] Unlike similar provisions concerning enforcement of environmental standards through port State control in other international instruments, Article 3(3) of the BWM Convention is exclusively linked to compliance with BWM Convention standards *within the internal waters* of States Parties.[304] Article 3(3) of the BWM Convention is thus perfectly in line with Article 34 of the Vienna Convention on the Law of Treaties.[305]

The BWM Convention assumes a very broad, functional understanding of a ship: According to Article 1(12) of the BWM Convention, a "ship" is a "vessel

---

A. Holljesiefken, *Die rechtliche Regulierung invasiver gebietsfremder Arten in Deutschland: Bestandsaufnahme und Bewertung* (Springer: Heidelberg, 2007), at 109.

298 IMO, Comprehensive Information on the Status of Multilateral Conventions and Instruments in Respect of which the International Maritime Organization or its Secretary-General Performs Depositary or Other Functions, 2 March 2021, <https://www.imo.org/en/About/Conventions/Pages/StatusOfConventions.aspx> (accessed 7 March 2021), at 524–528.

299 BWM Convention, Art. 3(1)(a).

300 BWM Convention, Art. 3(1)(b).

301 Cf. Proelß and Schatz (n. 24), at 86.

302 BWM Convention, Art. 3(3).

303 Zink (n. 285), at 110–111.

304 Ibid., at 211–215; Proelß and Schatz (n. 24), at 86.

305 VCLT (n. 204).

of any type whatsoever operating in the aquatic environment and includes submersibles, floating craft, floating platforms, FSUs and FPSOs". Nonetheless, several categories of ships are excluded from the application of the BWM Convention.[306] First, the Convention does not apply to ships that are not designed or built to carry ballast water.[307] Second, ships of a State Party operating exclusively in waters under the jurisdiction of that State Party do not fall within the scope of the BWM Convention unless that State Party determines that the discharge of ballast water from such ships would adversely affect or cause damage to the environment, human health, property or resources within its jurisdiction or that of neighbouring or other States.[308] Third, the BWM Convention does not apply to vessels of a State Party that operate only in waters under the jurisdiction of another State Party, subject to the latter State Party's authorization for such exclusion.[309] A State Party may not grant such authorization "if doing so would impair or damage its environment, human health, property or resources, or those of adjacent or other States".[310] Any State Party which does not grant such an authorization shall inform the administration of the ship concerned that the BWM Convention applies to that ship.[311] Fourth, ships (with the exception of ships that have not been granted a licence under Article 3(2)(c) of the BWM Convention) operating only in waters under the jurisdiction of a single State Party and on the high seas are also not subject to the requirements of the BWM Convention, unless the State Party concerned determines that the discharge of ballast water from such ships would "impair or damage their environment, human health, property or resources, or those of adjacent or other States".[312] Fifth, the BWM Convention does not apply to warships, naval auxiliaries or other ships "owned or operated by a State and used, for the time being, only on government non-commercial service".[313] However, each Party shall ensure, through appropriate measures that do not impair their operations or operational capabilities, that such ships act in a manner consistent with the BWM Convention (even though only "so far as is reasonable and practicable").[314] Finally, the BWM Convention does not apply to ballast water

306 Zink (n. 285), at 204–210.
307 BWM Convention, Art. 3(2)(a).
308 BWM Convention, Art. 3(2)(b).
309 BWM Convention, Art. 3(2)(c).
310 Ibid.
311 Ibid.
312 BWM Convention, Art. 3(2)(d).
313 BWM Convention, Art. 3(2)(e).
314 Ibid.

that is permanently carried in sealed tanks on ships and that is, therefore, not subject to discharge.[315]

It should be stressed that, according to Article 2(3) of the BWM Convention, "[n]othing in this Convention shall be interpreted as preventing a Party from taking, individually or jointly with other Parties, more stringent measures with respect to the prevention, reduction or elimination of the transfer of Harmful Aquatic Organisms and Pathogens through the control and management of ships' Ballast Water and Sediments, consistent with international law". Therefore, the BWM Convention does not regulate the issue of ballast water conclusively, as it does not prevent the adoption of stricter measures on, for example, the regional or national level.[316] This is of relevance with regard to the EU law instruments analyzed below.

#### 4.1.2.2 *Discharge of Ballast Water*

The term "ballast water" is defined in Article 1(2) of the BWM Convention as "water with its suspended matter taken on board a ship to control trim, list, draught, stability or stresses of the ship". According to Regulation A-2 of the Annex to the BWM Convention, the discharge of ballast water is only permitted as part of ballast water treatment as specified in the Annex to the BWM Convention, unless expressly provided otherwise. Thus, the Convention establishes a general prohibition of discharge of ballast water unless the requirements of the BWM Convention are met. The BWM Convention regime concerning the discharge of ballast water – and the permissibility of such discharges – is essentially based on two standards defined in the Annex to the BWM Convention, namely Regulation D-1 for ballast water exchange and Regulation D-2 for ballast water treatment.[317]

In order to meet the standard laid down in Regulation D-1, which is intended as an interim standard available until the entry into force of the standard in Regulation D-2,[318] a simple ballast water exchange is sufficient where an efficiency of at least 95% volumetric exchange of ballast water is achieved.[319] If ballast water is exchanged using the pumping-through method, pumping through three times the volume of each ballast water tank shall be "considered"

315 BWM Convention, Art. 3(2)(f).

316 Cf. Tsimplis (n. 296), at 417; D. Vidas and M. Markovčić Kostelac, 'Ballast Water and Alien Species: Regulating Global Transfers and Regional Consequences', in D. Vidas and P. J. Schei (eds.), *The World Ocean in Globalisation* (Martinus Nijhoff Publishers/Brill: Leiden/Boston, 2011), 371–392, at 389–390; Proelß and Schatz (n. 24), at 87.

317 For detailed analysis, see Zink (n. 285), at 215–237.

318 Ibid., at 216–222.

319 BWM Convention, Annex, Regulation D-1.1.

(as part of a legal fiction) to fulfil the 95%-rule.[320] If the volume of a ballast water tank is pumped through less than three times, this presumption does not apply and, accordingly, such practice may only be accepted if the ship can demonstrate that the 95%-rule is fulfilled as a matter of fact.[321]

Regulation B-4.1.1 provides that ballast water exchanges must, whenever possible, be conducted at least 200 nm from the nearest land and in waters at least 200 m in depth, taking into account the guidelines of the IMO. There are exceptions to this rule under Regulations B-4.1.2 and B-4.3 to B-4.4, but the reasons for any such use of exceptions by a ship must be registered in the ballast water record book in accordance with regulation B-4.5. In sea areas where the distance and depth criteria of Regulation B-4.1.1 cannot be met, Regulation B-4.2 provides for the possibility for port States (in consultation with adjacent or other States, as appropriate) to establish ballast water exchange areas deviating from Regulation B-4.1.1. For this purpose, the Marine Environmental Protection Committee (MEPC) of the IMO adopted the so-called G14 Guidelines, which prescribe how such areas are to be identified and defined.[322] On this basis, the Contracting Parties to the 1992 Convention for the Protection of the Marine Environment of the North-East Atlantic (OSPAR Convention)[323] designated a ballast water exchange area for traffic confined to the North Sea.[324] Vessels engaged in trade confined to the North Sea are required to carry out ballast water exchanges in the designated North Sea exchange area.[325] However, this only applies if the ballast water exchange area is located on a vessel's intended route.[326] Vessels are not obliged to deviate from their planned route or to delay the voyage in order to carry out a ballast water exchange.[327] No such exchange area has been designated for the Baltic Sea.[328]

---

320 BWM Convention, Annex, Regulation D-1.2.

321 Ibid.

322 IMO Marine Environment Protection Committee Resolution MEPC.151(55), of 13 October 2006, *Guidelines on Designation of Areas for Ballast Water Exchange (G14)*.

323 *Convention for the Protection of the Marine Environment of the North-East Atlantic*, adopted 22 September 1992, entered into force 25 March 1998, 2354 UNTS 67.

324 IMO BWM.2/Circ.56, of 13 July 2015, *Communication Received from the Government of the Netherlands*.

325 Ibid.

326 Ibid.

327 Ibid.

328 HELCOM, 'HELCOM Guide to Alien Species and Ballast Water Management in the Baltic Sea' (2014), <https://helcom.fi/wp-content/uploads/2019/08/HELCOM-Guide-to-Alien-Species-and-Ballast-Water-Management-in-the-Baltic-Sea.pdf> (accessed 17 November 2020), 22.

In accordance with Regulation B-3, the D-1 standard will apply to existing ships during a transitional period after the entry into force of the BWM Convention. The transition period during which the D-1 standard applies differs, among other things, according to the year of construction and the ballast water capacity of ships. However, due to the static transition periods (2014 and 2016, respectively) established in Regulation B-3, this standard expired before the BWM Convention entered into force in 2017.[329] For this reason, the IMO amended the D-1 standard by means of various resolutions in order to ensure the success of the BWM Convention. It is beyond the scope of this study to discuss these detailed regulations.[330] Following a resolution adopted by the IMO in 2017 to amend Regulation B-3, the transition periods were adjusted.[331] They now run until 8 September 2024 at the latest, irrespective of the type of ship.[332]

After the respective transition period, the standard of Regulation D-2 applies to newly built *and* existing ships.[333] This standard represents the main innovation and the progress made by the BWM Convention compared to the previously widespread practice of ballast water exchange.[334] It defines stricter quality standards for ballast water, compliance with which can only be ensured by a Ballast Water Management System (BWMS). Such systems usually use either mechanical-physical methods (e.g., irradiation with UV light), chemical methods (e.g., the use of biocides such as chlorine or chlorine dioxide) or a combination of such methods.[335] Especially when chemical methods are used, by-products of the disinfection process may develop in the treated ballast water.

Pursuant to Regulation D-2.1, when treated and subsequently discharged by BWMS, ballast water must contain concentrations of "less than 10 viable organisms per cubic metre greater than or equal to 50 micrometres in minimum dimension and less than 10 viable organisms per millilitre less than 50 micrometres in minimum dimension and greater than or equal to 10 micrometres in minimum dimension". In addition, in accordance with Regulation D-2.1, the concentration of indicator microbes (toxigenic *Vibrio cholerae*, *Escherichia coli*

329 Zink (n. 285), at 233–243.

330 For detailed discussion, see ibid.

331 IMO Marine Environment Protection Committee Resolution MEPC.287(71), of 7 July 2017, *Implementation of the BWM Convention* in conjunction with IMO Marine Environment Protection Committee Resolution MEPC 71/17/Add. 1 Annex 2, of 2017, *Draft Amendments to Regulation B-3 of the BWM Convention*.

332 Ibid.

333 Zink (n. 285), at 222–233.

334 Ibid.

335 Ibid., at 226–233.

and intestinal *Enterococci*) in the ballast water must not exceed the concentration described in Regulation D-2.2.

In order to ensure compliance with this standard, BWMS must be approved (so-called type-approval) by the competent authority of the flag State or a recognized classification society before they are installed and put into service.[336] This follows from the reference in Regulation D-3.1 to IMO Guidelines G8 and G9.[337] On the one hand, these guidelines lay down the general approval procedure which must be completed before a type-approval can be granted (IMO Guideline G-8); on the other hand, IMO Guideline G-9 prescribes complex requirements for BWMS that work with active substances. The use of such systems requires, among other things, the conduct of a separate risk analysis, which takes into account, *inter alia*, any by-products of the disinfection process contained in the treated ballast water.[338] Only those systems that can be qualified as safe on the basis of this risk analysis will receive a type-approval.

Regulation A-3 provides for various exceptions to the standards under Regulations D-1 and D-2. One exception concerns the uptake or discharge of ballast water and sediment "necessary for the purpose of ensuring the safety of a ship in emergency situations or saving life at sea".[339] Another exception refers to accidental ingress or discharge of ballast water and sediments as a result of damage to the ship or its equipment.[340] There is also an exception for the uptake and discharge of ballast water and sediments "when being used for the purpose of avoiding or minimizing pollution incidents from the ship".[341] A further exception applies when the same ballast water and sediments are taken up and subsequently discharged on the high seas.[342] Finally, an exception applies to the discharge of ballast water and sediment "from a ship at the same location where the whole of that [ballast water] and those [sediments] originated and provided that no mixing with unmanaged [ballast water] and [sediments] from other areas has occurred".[343] This exception does not apply, of course, if mixing has taken place.[344]

---

336 IMO (n. 10).

337 IMO Marine Environment Protection Committee Resolution MEPC.279(70), of 28 October 2016, *Guidelines for Approval of Ballast Water Management Systems (G8)*; IMO Marine Environment Protection Committee Resolution MEPC.169(57), of 4 April 2008, *Procedure for Approval of Ballast Water Management Systems that Make Use of Active Substances (G9)*.

338 For the detailed discussion, see Zink (n. 285), at 289–298.

339 BWM Convention, Annex, Regulation A-3.1.

340 BWM Convention, Annex, Regulation A-3.2.

341 BWM Convention, Annex, Regulation A-3.3.

342 BWM Convention, Annex, Regulation A-3.4.

343 BWM Convention, Annex, Regulation A-3.5.

344 Ibid.

In order to ensure compliance with the standards of the BWM Convention and to facilitate inspections by port States, all ships are required to carry documents. According to Regulation B-1, which is further specified by the IMO's Guidelines for Ballast Water Management and Development of Ballast Water Management Plans (G4 Guidelines),[345] every ship, regardless of its size, must carry a ballast water management plan on board. This management plan contains a description of the technical characteristics of the ship and an adapted instruction manual which specifies the ballast water management required for the ship concerned in order to ensure compliance with the BWM Convention's ballast water quality standards.[346] Pursuant to Regulation B-2, all ships are required to keep a ballast water record book on board to document the information relevant for compliance with the BWM Convention's ballast water standards. This record book must contain records of all relevant procedures, including discharges of ballast water.[347]

#### 4.1.2.3 *Discharge or Disposal of Sediments*

According to Article 1(11) of the BWM Convention, the term "sediments" refers to "matter settled out of [ballast water] within a ship". Pursuant to Regulation B-5.1 of the Annex to the BWM Convention, all ships are required to remove and dispose of sediment from spaces designated to carry ballast water in accordance with the ship's ballast water management plan. In principle, however, the BWM Convention does not prescribe separate standards for the handling of sediments. Instead, the fact that Article 1(3) of the BWM Convention includes sediments in the definition of "ballast water treatment" suggests that the same standard applies to sediments.[348] It is true that sediments are not expressly mentioned alongside ballast water in Regulation A-2, which lays down the prohibition of discharge, unless the standards under D-1 or D-2 are complied with or an exception applies. However, in any event, it follows – *a contrario* – from the exceptions in Regulation A-3 ("accidental discharge or ingress of Ballast Water *and Sediments*") that the discharge of sediments together with ballast water is also generally prohibited unless the relevant standards under Regulations D-1 or D-2 are complied with or an exception applies.[349] This conclusion seems logical given that the discharged ballast water usually contains at least small amounts of sediments.

---

345 IMO Marine Environment Protection Committee Resolution MEPC.127(53), of 22 July 2005, *Guidelines for Ballast Water Management and Development of Ballast Water Management Plans (G4)*.

346 For detailed discussion, see Zink (n. 285), at 269–272.

347 Ibid., at 273–274.

348 Ibid., at 277.

349 Ibid.

In contrast, the complete removal and disposal of sediments from ballast tanks is usually only possible in the shipyard. Therefore, para. 1.3.4 of the G4 Guidelines of the IMO, which specify Regulation B-5.1 of the Annex to the BWM Convention, stipulates that the removal and disposal of sediments from ballast tanks should be carried out on a timely basis in accordance with the ballast water management plan and as found necessary. The timing and frequency of these measures can be made dependent on various factors, such as the speed of sediment deposition or the availability of suitable reception facilities in ports. According to para. 1.3.5 of the G4 Guidelines, the measures should preferably be carried out under controlled conditions in a port, in a repair facility or in a dry dock. Furthermore, disposal should preferably take place in a reception facility for sediments from ballast tanks, if such facility is available and disposal reasonable and practical. In contrast, disposal at sea (which does *not* mean discharge together with the ballast water) should only be permissible according to para. 3.5 of the G4 Guidelines if the ship is located at a distance of at least 200 nm from land, and where the water depth is at least 200 m.

The BWM Convention pursues two further strategies to better avoid the dangers posed by sediments from ballast water tanks. The first strategy, which is laid down in Regulation B-5.2, focuses on the construction of ships and is intended to reduce the build-up of sediments. Newly constructed ships should in principle be designed and constructed in such a way as to minimize the intake and undesirable retention of sediment, and to facilitate its removal. They should also provide safe access for sediment removal and sampling taking into account guidelines developed by the IMO. The relevant guidelines are the 2012 IMO Guidelines on Design and Construction to Facilitate Sediment Control on Ships (G12).[350] Ships to which Regulation B-5.2 does not apply should nevertheless comply with this standard "to the extent practicable".[351]

The second strategy is to set up sediment reception facilities to ensure proper disposal. In this respect, Article 5(1) of the BWM Convention imposes an obligation on all States Parties to ensure that adequate sediment reception facilities are provided in or at ports and terminals where cleaning or repair work on ballast tanks takes place – once again taking into account the guidelines developed by the IMO. The 2006 IMO Guidelines for Sediment Reception Facilities

350 IMO Marine Environment Protection Committee Resolution MEPC.209(63), of 2 March 2012, *Guidelines on Design and Construction to Facilitate Sediment Control on Ships* (G12).

351 BWM Convention, Annex, Regulation B-5.2 in conjuction with Regulation B-3.1.

(G1) are relevant in this respect.[352] As noted above, the BWM Convention does not contain any provision stipulating that ballast water sediments must be disposed of exclusively in such reception facilities.[353] However, para. 1.4 of the G1 Guidelines expressly recognizes that some States have already introduced national regulations for the disposal of ship-generated waste, which may also be extended to the disposal of ballast water sediments. Indeed, as shown by Article 2(3) of the BWM Convention, the BWM Convention regime does not preclude such regulations, including where they impose an obligation to dispose of waste in reception facilities in connection with a ban on discharge.

### 4.2 *EU Legislation concerning the Discharge of Ballast Water*

The BWM Convention is currently implemented directly by its States Parties, not by the EU. The EU has not yet enacted detailed regulation with respect to the issue of ballast water.[354] Nor can the EU itself become a party to the BWM Convention, since Article 17(1) of the BWM Convention only permits States to become Parties.[355] Against this background, Recital 21 of the EU's Regulation on the Prevention and Management of the Introduction and Spread of Invasive Alien Species (IAS Regulation)[356] merely calls upon the EU Commission to "take all appropriate steps to encourage Member States to ratify [the BWM Convention]". Other EU law instruments also pay attention to safeguard their compatibility with the BWM Convention, without, however, taking the issue of ballast water management any further in terms of regulation. For example, Recital 24 of the EU's Regulation concerning the Placing on the Market and Use of Biocidal Products (Biocidal Products Regulation)[357] states:

> As the [BWM Convention] provides for an effective assessment of the risks posed by ballast water management systems, the final approval and

352 IMO Marine Environment Protection Committee Resolution MEPC.152(55), of 13 October 2006, *Guidelines for Sediment Reception Facilities (G1)*.

353 Zink (n. 285), at 278.

354 EMSA, 'Ballast Water' 2020, at: <http://emsa.europa.eu/implementation-tasks/environment/ballast-water.html> (accessed 17 November 2020).

355 On the role of the EU, see Zink (n. 285), at 446–462.

356 Regulation (EU) No. 1143/2014 of the European Parliament and of the Council of 22 October 2014 on the Prevention and Management of the Introduction and Spread of Invasive Alien Species OJ L 317/35.

357 Regulation (EU) No. 528/2012 of the European Parliament and of the Council of 22 May 2012 concerning the Making Available on the Market and Use of Biocidal Products OJ L 167/1.

> subsequent type-approval of such systems should be considered equivalent to the product authorisation required under this Regulation.

Accordingly, Article 2(6) of the Biocidal Products Regulation stipulates that "[b]iocidal products which obtained final approval under the [BWM Convention] shall be considered as authorised under Chapter VIII of this Regulation".

Although the EU has not implemented the BWM Convention within the EU legal system, some legislative acts of the Union are relevant to the question of the legality of discharges of ballast water and sediments from ballast water tanks. In particular, the MSFD and the WFD should be mentioned here.[358] In principle, it can be said that the BWM Convention contributes to the achievement of the objectives prescribed in the MSFD and the implementation measures taken by the EU Member States.[359] However, with regard to the specific question of the discharge of *treated* ballast water, a conflict between the BWM Convention and the objectives of the MSFD cannot entirely be ruled out. This is because the treatment of ballast water under the D-2 standard also involves the use of chemicals such as chlorine and chlorine dioxide, which, together with any by-products of the disinfection process, could have a negative impact on the water quality in case of increased concentration, despite the risk assessment that has been carried out.[360] It should be kept in mind, though, that the MSFD does not stipulate a prohibition of deterioration to be implemented by the EU Member States. Article 1(2)(a) of the MSFD merely requires that marine strategies are developed and implemented to protect and preserve the marine environment and prevent its deterioration. Therefore, it cannot be assumed that the MSFD prohibits, in an absolute fashion, any adverse change in the state of marine waters.[361] In contrast, Article 4(1)(a)(i) of the WFD indeed stipulates a deterioration ban with a view to the status of surface waters, which must be observed by EU Member State authorities in the context of the granting of permits for specific activities.

### 4.3 *Relationship between Applicable International Law and EU Law*

In principle, the measures enacted by the EU applicable to discharges of ballast water are compatible with the pertinent international legal rules (i.e., in particular Article 196(1) of UNCLOS and the BWM Convention), at least in so far

358 See supra 2.2.3. and 2.2.4.

359 Cf. Zink (n. 285), at 452–453.

360 Ibid., at 487.

361 Proelß (n. 143), at [19]. Contra: M. Kotulla, '§ 45a', in M. Kotulla (ed.), *Wasserhaushaltsgesetz: Kommentar (2nd ed.)* (Kohlhammer: Stuttgart, 2011), [5].

as the reduction of the introduction of invasive species is concerned. However, if ballast water is treated with chemical methods according to Regulation D-2 of the Annex to the BWM Convention, the potentially resulting discharge of by-products of the disinfection process could raise problems with regard to its compatibility with the WFD. If and to the extent to which the BWM Convention were to conflict with the WFD, the WFD would take precedence within the legal systems of the EU Member States. It should be noted, though, that the BWM Convention, similar to Article 195 of UNCLOS (which, however, only applies to "pollution of the marine environment"), seeks to prevent transformations of one type of pollution into another that might be caused *by* the ballast water treatment processes.[362] The States Parties to the BWM Convention must thus ensure that ballast water treatment processes "do not cause greater harm than they prevent to their environment, human health, property or resources, or those of other States".[363] This implies that a conflict with the WFD is avoidable through interpretation, at least at the level of implementation, i.e. within the framework of the domestic laws of the EU Member States.[364]

## 4.4 *Concluding Observations*

According to the BWM Convention, the discharge of ballast water is only allowed when conducted in accordance with the Annex to the Convention, unless otherwise specified. The legal regime established by the BWM Convention is based on two standards: first, Regulation D-1 regarding ballast water exchange, and second, Regulation D-2 concerning ballast water treatment. Any exchange of ballast water has to be conducted at a distance of at least 200 nm from the nearest land and in water depths of at least 200 m, and must take into account the applicable guidelines of the IMO. The D-1 standard is merely a transitional solution for existing ships. In 2017, the IMO adjusted the transition periods depending on the year of construction and the ballast capacity of the ship concerned, making clear that the D-1 standard cannot be applied, independently of the type of vessel, after 9 September 2024. The standard provided by Regulation D-2 applies to new ships and existing ships after the transition period under Regulation D-1 has expired. Regulation D-2 comprises stricter quality standards for ballast water, which can only be met by way of using BWMS. However, in the application of the D-2 standard, by-products of disinfection processes may form in the processed ballast water particularly when chemical methods are used.

362 Proelß and Schatz (n. 24), at 93.
363 BWM Convention, Art. 2(7).
364 Proelß and Schatz (n. 24), at 93.

Regulation D-2.1 contains requirements concerning the maximum concentration and size of viable organisms, and indicator microbes per cubic meter of ballast water. To ensure compliance with these requirements, BWMS need to be licensed in terms of a type-approval by the flag State's competent authorities or a recognized classification society before being installed and put into operation. The basic approval procedure and requirements concerning BWMS, if operating with active substances, are laid down in IMO Guidelines G8 and G9. Operating such systems requires, *inter alia*, the implementation of a risk analysis which ought to take into account the potential formation of disinfection by-products in the ballast water. Only systems that can, based on the risk analysis, be considered as unproblematic may be granted a type-approval.

So far, ballast water has not been subject to detailed EU regulation. Regardless of this, however, EU Member States must act in accordance with the requirements set out in EU law – especially the MSFD and WFD – when implementing the BWM Convention.

## 5 Conclusion

This analysis has shown that the regulation of vessel discharges is characterized by extraordinary complexity and high technicality. A particular challenge results from the fact that the relevant regulations are found at different levels of law and contained in a large number of legal instruments which are, again, partly based on different regulatory approaches. In Europe, which has served as a regional case-study for the purposes of this analysis, additional difficulties arise from the fact that EU law represents a further level of law that comes alongside international law and national law. This additional level of law is characterized by overarching and broad regulatory approaches which set binding management objectives and oblige the Member States to develop strategies to achieve good water status (WFD and MSFD). In some cases, these approaches are then supplemented by specific instruments (e.g., the Sulphur Directive and Directive on Port Reception Facilities). In order to avoid repetition of the detailed concluding observations provided in each chapter, this conclusion focuses on notable general and overarching observations.[365]

On the level of public international law, all three categories of vessel discharges examined in this study are regulated by multilateral treaties of global application that have been adopted under the auspices of the IMO. The management of both scrubber washwater discharges and sewage discharges is

365 See supra 2.4., 3.4., and 4.4.

primarily regulated within the framework of the MARPOL Convention – in Annexes VI and IV, respectively. The management of ballast water has not made its way into the MARPOL Convention framework, but has been addressed by way of adoption of a new international agreement, the BWM Convention. A key difference between the categories of discharges analyzed in this study is that scrubber washwater discharges – as the result of an alternative method of reducing SOx emissions of vessels – constitute a transfer of one form of pollution into another (cf. Article 195 of UNCLOS), whereas sewage and ballast water discharges are the result of the traditional operation of ships. At the same time, ballast water on the one hand, and scrubber washwater and sewage on the other can be distinguished by referring to the fact that ballast water *must* be discharged in order to operate traditional ships, whereas discharges of washwater and sewage are not necessary and may be prevented through suitable technologies.

All three regulatory frameworks remain dynamic at the global and regional levels. First, the regulation of scrubber washwater discharges, which consists of an innovative set of rules created in the context of stricter SOx emission limits, may well develop towards a ban of open loop scrubbers at least within the waters of many coastal States as scientific knowledge about the negative environmental impacts of such discharges increases. At present, the EU, whether intentionally or not, has gone beyond the requirements of international law in its regulatory efforts by establishing a legal obligation of the Member States to permit in their domestic legislation the use of emission reduction methods that fulfill the conditions set out in the Sulphur Directive, including open loop scrubbers. In this respect, the Sulphur Directive conflicts with the CDNI, which applies in the inland waterways of some (but not all) EU Member States, and which prohibits discharges of scrubber washwater – albeit not as a result of intentional regulation but due to the lack of provisions exempting such discharges from the absolute prohibition of discharges under the CDNI. This is regrettable given that a prohibition of scrubber washwater discharges in inland waterways would better serve to fulfill the objectives of the Directive on Port Reception Facilities, the WFD and the MSFD than the present approach of the Sulphur Directive.

Second, with respect to sewage discharges, additional restrictions are being adopted and existing exemptions are being removed to avoid eutrophication of sensitive marine environments, of which the additional requirements of Annex IV to the HELCOM Convention in the Baltic Sea region are a good example. However, some of these requirements conflict with the CDNI insofar as inland waterways are concerned – with the difference that, here, the CDNI is less restrictive than Annex IV to the HELCOM Convention. Again, a resolution of this conflict by consistently adopting a broad prohibition of sewage discharges would best serve the objectives of the Directive on Port Reception Facilities, the WFD and the MSFD.

Third, in respect of ballast water discharges, further developments are inherent in the framework of the BWM Convention, which is based on two standards: first, Regulation D-1 regarding ballast water exchange, and second, Regulation D-2 concerning ballast water treatment. Currently, the D-1 standard is being applied as a transitional solution for existing ships until 9 September 2024. After this date, both existing and new ships must comply with the D-2 standard unless there is another extension of the transition period. But even under the stricter quality standards of Regulation D-2, which can only be met by way of using BWMS, ballast water discharges may have environmental impacts – only this time for the water quality (e.g., due to disinfectants and chemical used to treat ballast water) rather than due to the introduction of invasive alien species. While there is no special regulation of ballast water management under EU law, EU Member States must act in accordance with the requirements set out in the MSFD and WFD when implementing the BWM Convention.

It may thus be concluded that many difficulties of vessel discharge regulation are related to the fact that seaports are often located in inland waterways, which means that seagoing vessels literally navigate the different but overlapping legal frameworks applicable in marine and freshwater areas. It is therefore essential that the relevant regulatory instruments are coordinated to the greatest extent possible in order to avoid inconsistencies and regime collisions. Only then can it be guaranteed that the category of marine pollution from ships examined in this study can be addressed by way of coherent and effective application of the law. Given the regrettable state of marine and freshwater environments in many areas subject to high vessel traffic, the proposed coherent regulation should be as restrictive as possible – without being prohibitively restrictive for international shipping.

## Acknowledgments

This monograph is a translated, updated and substantially revised text originally prepared by the authors as a legal expert opinion for the German Environment Agency (Umweltbundesamt – UBA) in 2019 (Proelß, A. and Schatz, V. (2019), Rechtliche Vorgaben zum Umgang mit Schiffsabwasser: Völker-, unions- und nationalrechtliche Anforderungen an Einleitungen von Scrubber-Abwasser, Ballastwasser und häuslichem Abwasser durch Schiffe (Dessau-Roßlau: Umweltbundesamt, Texte | 09/2019). The authors would like to thank Emma Bartmann, Christopher Janz, Rahel Schwarz and Sara Wissmann, all of them student research assistants at the Chair for the International Law of the Sea and International Environmental Law, Public International Law and Public Law of the University of Hamburg, for their support in finalizing this project.

## List of References

### *Bibliography*

Bang, H. 'Port State Jurisdiction and Article 218 of the UN Convention on the Law of Sea' (2009) 40 *Journal of Maritime Law and Commerce* 291.

Bartenstein, K. 'Article 211', in A. Proelss (ed.), *United Nations Convention on the Law of the Sea (UNCLOS): A Commentary* (C. H. Beck/Hart/Nomos: Munich/Oxford/Baden-Baden, 2017), 1419–1443.

den Boer, E. and M. Hoen, *Scrubbers: An Economic and Ecological Assessment* (CE Delft, 2015).

Callies, C. 'Art. 193 AEUV', in C. Callies and M. Ruffert (eds.), *EUV/AEUV: Das Verfassungsrecht der Europäischen Union mit Europäischer Grundrechtecharta: Kommentar (5th ed.)* (C. H. Beck: München, 2016).

Christodoulou-Varotsi, I. *Maritime Safety Law and Policies of the European Union and the United States of America: Antagonism or Synergy?* (Springer: Berlin, 2009).

Coelho, N. F. *Unilateral Port State Jurisdiction: The Quest for Universality in the Prevention, Reduction and Control of Ship-source Pollution* (Utrecht University, 2019), https://www.uu.nl/sites/default/files/rebo-nelson-coelho-54375_thesis-ilovepdf-compressed.pdf (accessed 7 March 2021).

Czybulka, D. 'Article 192', in A. Proelss (ed.), *United Nations Convention on the Law of the Sea (UNCLOS): A Commentary* (C. H. Beck/Hart/Nomos: Munich/Oxford/Baden-Baden, 2017), 1277–1287.

Czybulka, D. 'Article 196', in A. Proelss (ed.), United Nations Convention on the Law of the Sea (UNCLOS): A Commentary (C. H. Beck/Hart/Nomos: Munich/Oxford/Baden-Baden, 2017), 1319–1328.

Faber, J., B. van Hattum and F. Kleissen, *The Impacts of EGCS Washwater Discharges on Port Water and Sediment* (CE Delft, 2019).

Fonseva de Souza Rolim, M. H. *The International Law on Ballast Water: Preventing Biopollution* (Martinus Nijhoff Publishers: Leiden/Boston, 2008).

Frank, V. *The European Community and Marine Environmental Protection in the International Law of the Sea: Implementing Global Obligations at the Regional Level* (Martinus Nijhoff Publishers: Leiden, 2007).

Freestone, D. 'International Fisheries Law since Rio: The Continued Rise of the Precautionary Principle', in: A. E. Boyle and D. Freestone (eds.), *International Law and Sustainable Development: Past Achievements and Future Challenges* (Oxford University Press, 1999), 135–164.

Gilek, M. and K. Kern (eds.), *Governing Europe's Marine Environment: Europeanization of Regional Seas or Regionalisation of EU Policies?* (Routledge: Abingdon, 2015).

Harrison, J. *Saving the Oceans Through Law: The International Legal Framework for the Protection of the Marine Environment* (Oxford University Press, 2017).

Holljesiefken, A. *Die rechtliche Regulierung invasiver gebietsfremder Arten in Deutschland: Bestandsaufnahme und Bewertung* (Springer: Heidelberg, 2007).

Höltmann, M. *Schiffssicherheit und Meeresumweltschutz in der EU nach Erika und Prestige: Die Vereinbarkeit der Gesetzesmaßnahmen der EU mit dem internationalen Seerecht* (Nomos: Baden-Baden, 2012).

Honniball, A. 'Singapore: Precautionary Unilateralism: Port State Prohibition on Open-Loop Scrubber Discharges and the IMO 2020 Fuel Oil Sulphur Limit' (2019) 4 *Asia-Pacific Journal of Ocean Law and Policy* 270.

Käller, A. 'Art. 193 AEUV', in J. Schwarze, U. Becker, A. Hatje et al (eds.), *EU-Kommentar (4th ed.)* (Nomos: Baden-Baden, 2019).

Karim, M. S. *Prevention of Pollution of the Marine Environment from Vessels: The Potential and Limits of the International Maritime Organisation* (Springer: New York, 2015).

Kjølholt, J., S. Aakre, C. Jürgensen et al., *Assessment of Possible Impacts of Scrubber Water Discharges on the Marine Environment* (Miljøstyrelsen: Copenhagen, 2012).

Kohen, M. 'Is the Internal Waters Regime Excluded from the United Nations Convention on the Law of the Sea?', in L. del Castillo (ed.), *Law of the Sea, From Grotius to the International Tribunal for the Law of the Sea: Liber Amicorum Judge Hugo Caminos* (Brill: Leiden, 2015), 110–124.

Kotulla, M. '§ 45a', in M. Kotulla (ed.), *Wasserhaushaltsgesetz: Kommentar (2nd ed.)* (Kohlhammer: Stuttgart, 2011).

Krämer, L. 'Art. 193 AEUV', in H. von der Groeben, J. Schwarze and A. Hatje (eds.), *Europäisches Unionsrecht (7th ed.)* (Nomos: Baden-Baden, 2015).

Lange, B., T. Markus and Lutz P. Helfst, *Impacts of Scrubbers on the Environmental Situation in Ports and Coastal Waters* (Umweltbundesamt: Dessau-Roßlau, 2014).

Markus, T. and L. P. Helfst, 'Regulierung der Einleitung von Abwasser aus Schiffsabgasreinigungsanlagen zum Schutz der Meere' (2014) 36 *Natur und Recht* 760.

Marr, S. *The Precautionary Principle in the Law of the Sea: Modern Decision Making in International Law* (Martinus Nijhoff: Leiden, 2003).

Nettesheim, M. 'Art. 193 AEUV', in E. Grabitz, M. Hilf and M. Nettesheim (eds.), *Das Recht der Europäischen Union: EUV/AEUV (71th ed.)* (C. H. Beck: München, 2020).

Nordquist, M. H., N. R. Grandy, S. Rosenne et al (eds.), *United Nations Convention on the Law of the Sea 1982: A Commentary*, Vol. 4 (Martinus Nijhoff: Dordrecht: 1991).

Proelss, A. 'Article 56', in A. Proelss (ed.), *United Nations Convention on the Law of the Sea (UNCLOS): A Commentary* (C. H. Beck/Hart/Nomos: Munich/Oxford/Baden-Baden, 2017), 418–437.

Proelss, A. 'Dispute Settlement in Multi-Layered Constellations: International Law and the EU' (2014) 57 *German Yearbook of International Law* 225.

Proelß, A. 'Article 43 WHG', in M. Beckmann, W. Durner, T. Mann et al (eds.), *Landmann/ Rohmer: Umweltrecht: Kommentar* (92nd ed.) (C. H. Beck: Munich, 2020).

Proelß, A. '§ 45a WHG', in M. Beckmann, W. Durner, T. Mann et al (eds.), *Landmann/ Rohmer: Umweltrecht: Kommentar* (92nd ed.) (C. H. Beck: Munich, 2020).

Proelß, A. *Meeresschutz im Völker- und Europarecht: Das Beispiel des Nordostatlantiks* (Duncker & Humblot: Berlin, 2004).

Proelß, A. and V. J. Schatz, 'Einleitungen von Schiffsabwasser aus Abgasreinigungsanlagen: Eine rechtliche Bestandsaufnahme' (2019) 30 *Zeitschrift für Umweltrecht* 592.

Proelß, A. and V. J. Schatz, *Rechtliche Vorgaben zum Umgang mit Schiffsabwasser: Völker-, unions- und nationalrechtliche Anforderungen an Einleitungen von Scrubber-Abwasser, Ballastwasser und häuslichem Abwasser durch Schiffe* (Umweltbundesamt: Dessau-Roßlau, 2019).

Reimann, M. *Binnenschiffahrt, Umweltrecht und Gewässerschutz im nationalen und internationalen Kontext* (Nomos: Baden-Baden, 1999).

Ringbom, H. *The EU Maritime Safety Policy and International Law* (Martinus Nijhoff Publishers: Leiden, 2008).

Ringbom, H., B. Bohman and S. Ilvessalo, *Combatting Eutrophication in the Baltic Sea: Legal Aspects of Sea-Based Engineering Measures* (Brill: Leiden, 2018).

Rothwell, D. R. and T. Stephens, *The International Law of the Sea*, 2nd ed. (Hart Publishing: Oxford and Portland, 2016).

Royal Society, 'Ocean Acidification Due to Increasing Atmospheric Carbon Dioxide' (2005), at: <https://royalsociety.org/~/media/Royal_Society_Content/policy/publications/2005/9634.pdf> (accessed 17 November 2020).

Sage-Fuller, B. *The Precautionary Principle in Marine Environmental Law: With Special Reference to High Risk Vessels* (Routledge: London, 2015).

Schminke, V. *Die Einleitung häuslicher Schiffsabwässer nach nationalem und internationalem Recht* (Peter Lang: Frankfurt am Main, 2009).

Shi, Y. 'China's First Local Regulation on Air Pollution from Vessels: An Appraisal' (2020) 5 *Asia-Pacific Journal of Ocean Law and Policy* 222.

Solf, K. *Europäisches Meeresumweltrecht im Internationalen Mehrebenensystem: Grenzen und Möglichkeiten eines europäischen Meeresumweltrechts am Beispiel europäischer und internationaler Vorgaben zur Eindämmung von Schiffsemissionen* (Nomos: Baden-Baden, 2017).

Stephens, T. 'Article 198', in A. Proelss (ed.), *United Nations Convention on the Law of the Sea (UNCLOS): A Commentary* (C. H. Beck/Hart/Nomos: Munich/Oxford/ Baden-Baden, 2017), 1333–1338.

Stöfen-O'Brien, A. *The International and European Legal Regime Regulating Marine Litter in the EU* (Nomos: Baden-Baden, 2015).

Tanaka, Y. 'Article 1', in A. Proelss (ed.), *United Nations Convention on the Law of the Sea (UNCLOS): A Commentary* (C. H. Beck/Hart/Nomos: Munich/Oxford/Baden-Baden, 2017), 17–26.

Teuchies, J., T. J. S. Cox, K. van Itterbeeck et al., 'The Impact of Scrubber Discharge on the Water Quality in Estuaries and Ports' (2020) 32 *Environmental Sciences Europe*, <https://doi.org/10.1186/s12302-020-00380-z> (accessed 17 November 2020).

Tsimplis, M. 'Alien Species Stay Home: The International Convention for the Management of Ships' Ballast Water and Sediments 2004' (2005) 19 *International Journal of Marine and Coastal Law* 411.

Vidas, D. and M. Markovčić Kostelac, 'Ballast Water and Alien Species: Regulating Global Transfers and Regional Consequences', in D. Vidas and P. J. Schei (eds.), *The World Ocean in Globalisation* (Martinus Nijhoff Publishers/Brill: Leiden/Boston, 2011), 371–392.

Windemuth, N. *Meeresverschmutzung durch den internationalen Seeverkehr: Ausweitung staatlicher Kontroll- und Interventionsrechte zum Schutz der Meeresumwelt* (Peter Lang: Frankfurt am Main, 2011).

Yang, H. C., J. Cha, S. Kim et al., 'Entry Into Force of Ship Ballast Water Management Convention and Its Implementation from Perspective of Northeast Asia' (2017) 1 *Journal of International Maritime Safety, Environmental Affairs, and Shipping* 19.

Zink, A. R. *Das Ballastwasser-Übereinkommen der internationalen Seeschifffahrts-Organisation von 2004: Anwendung in Nord- und Ostsee* (Nomos: Baden-Baden, 2016).

Zink, A. 'The IMO's Ballast Water Management Convention of 2004: A Decade of Evolution and Challenges' (2015) 29 *Ocean Yearbook* 441.

### *Treaties*

*Convention on Biological Diversity*, adopted 5 June 1992, entered into force 29 December 1993, 1760 UNTS 79.

*Convention on the Collection, Deposit and Reception of Waste Generated During Navigation on the Rhine and Other Inland Waterways*, adopted 9 September 1996, entered into force 1 November 2009, Overheid Treaty Database, at: <https://treatydatabase.overheid.nl/en/Verdrag/Details/007367.html> (accessed 17 November 2020).

*Convention on Long-range Transboundary Air Pollution*, adopted 13 November 1979, entered into force 16 March 1983, 1302 UNTS 217.

*Convention on the Prevention of Marine Pollution by Dumping of Wastes and Other Matter*, adopted 29 December 1972, entered into force 30 August 1975, 1046 UNTS 120.

*Convention on the Protection of the Marine Environment of the Baltic Sea*, adopted 9 April 1992, entered into force 3 May 1980, 2099 UNTS 195.

*Convention for the Protection of the Marine Environment of the North-East Atlantic*, adopted 22 September 1992, entered into force 25 March 1998, 2354 UNTS 67.

*Convention for the Safety of Life at Sea*, adopted 1 November 1974, entered into force 25 May 1980, 1184 UNTS 278.

*International Convention for the Control and Management of Ships' Ballast Water and Sediments*, adopted 13 February 2004, entered into force 8 September 2017, UNTS Reg. No. 55544.

*International Convention for the Prevention of Pollution of the Sea by Oil*, adopted 12 May 1954, entered into force 26 July 1958, 327 UNTS 3.

*International Convention for the Prevention of Pollution from Ships*, adopted 2 November 1973, entered into force 2 October 1983, 1340 UNTS 184.

*United Nations Convention on the Law of the Sea*, adopted 10 December 1982, entered into force 16 November 1994, 1833 UNTS 3.

*Protocol of 1978 relating to the International Convention for the Prevention of Pollution from Ships, 1973*, adopted 17 February 1978, entered into force 2 October 1983, 1340 UNTS 61.

*Protocol to the Convention on the Prevention of Marine Pollution by Dumping of Wastes and Other Matter, 1972*, adopted 7 November 1996, entered into force 24 March 2006, (1997) 36 ILM 1.

*Protocol to the 1979 Convention on Long-range Transboundary Air Pollution to Abate Acidification, Eutrophication and Ground-level Ozone*, adopted 30 November 1999, entered into force 17 May 2005, 2319 UNTS 81.

*Vienna Convention on the Law of Treaties*, adopted 23 May 1969, entered into force 27 January 1980, 1155 UNTS 331.

### *EU Law*

Directive (EC) 2000/60 of the European Parliament and of the Council of 23 October 2000 Establishing a Framework for Community Action in the Field of Water Policy OJ L 327/1.

Directive (EC) 2005/35 of the European Parliament and of the Council of 7 September 2005 on Ship-source Pollution and on the Introduction of Penalties for Infringements OJ L 255/11.

Directive (EC) 2008/56 of the European Parliament and of the Council of 17 June 2018 Establishing a Framework for Community Action in the Field of Marine Environmental Policy OJ L 164/19.

Directive (EC) 2008/98 of the European Parliament and of the Council of 19 November 2008 on Waste and Repealing certain Directives OJ L 312/3.

Directive (EU) 2012/33 of the European Parliament and of the Council of 21 November 2012 Amending Council Directive 1999/32/EC as Regards the Sulphur Content of Marine Fuels OJ L 327/1.

Directive (EU) 2013/39 of the European Parliament and of the Council of 12 August 2013 Amending Directives 2000/60/EC and 2008/105/EC as regards Priority Substances in the Field of Water Policy OJ L 226/1.

Directive (EU) 2015/1535 of the European Parliament and of the Council of 9 September 2015 Laying Down a Procedure for the Provision of Information in the Field of Technical Regulations and of Rules on Information Society Services OJ L 241/1.

Directive (EU) 2016/802 of the European Parliament and of the Council of 11 May 2016 concerning a Reduction in the Sulphur Content of Certain Liquid Fuels OJ L 132/58.

Directive (EU) 2019/883 of the European Parliament and of the Council of 17 April 2019 on Port Reception Facilities for the Delivery of Waste from Ships, Amending Directive (EU) 2010/65 and Repealing Directive 2000/59/EC OJ L 151/116.

Regulation (EU) No. 1143/2014 of the European Parliament and of the Council of 22 October 2014 on the Prevention and Management of the Introduction and Spread of Invasive Alien Species OJ L 317/35.

Regulation (EU) No. 528/2012 of the European Parliament and of the Council of 22 May 2012 concerning the Making Available on the Market and Use of Biocidal Products OJ L 167/1.

The Treaty on the Functioning of the European Union OJ C 326/47.

### *EU Documents*

EU Commission COM(2015) 120, of 9 March 2015, Communication from the Commission to the European Parliament and the Council, The Water Framework Directive and the Floods Directive: Actions Towards the 'Good Status' of EU Water and to Reduce Flood Risks.

EU Commission COM(2018) 188, of 16 April 2018, Report from the Commission to the European Parliament and the Council on Implementation and Compliance with the Sulphur Standards for Marine Fuels Set Out in Directive (EU) 2016/802 Relating to a Reduction in the Sulphur Content of Certain Liquid Fuels.

EU Commission COM(2018) 33 final, of 16 January 2018, Proposal for a Directive of the European Parliament and of the Council on Port Reception Facilities for Ship-generated waste, repealing Directive 2000/59/EC and amending Directives 2009/16/EC and 2010/65/EU.

EU Commission COM(2020) 259 final, of 25 June 2020, Report from the Commission to the European Parliament and the Council on the Implementation of the Marine Strategy Framework Directive (Directive 2008/56/EC).

EU Commission ENV.C.3/RH, of 18 January 2016, Commission's Views on the Discharge of Scrubber Wash Water and the Updated Table Summarising the Position of Member States on the Acceptability of Discharges of Scrubber Wash Water.

EU Parliament E-003307/2017, of 30 June 2017, Parliamentary Questions: Answer given by Mr Vella on behalf of the Commission to a Parliamentary Question posed by Jan Huitema on 2 June 2015.

European Sustainable Shipping Forum 3rd Plenary Meeting, of 4 December 2014, Final Report Submission from the ESSF Sub-Groups.

### *IMO, HELCOM and CDNI Documents*

CDNI Res. CDNI 2013-II-5, of 12 December 2013, *Dispositions Dérogatoires Pour Difficultés Insurmontables Conformément à l'Article 9.02 de l'Annexe 2 Pour Les Stations d'Épuration de Bord.*

HELCOM Recommendation 22/1, of 21 March 2001, *Installation of Toilet Retention Systems and Standard Connections for the Sewage on Board Existing Fishing Vessels, Working Vessels and Pleasure Craft.*

IMO BWM.2/Circ.56, of 13 July 2015, *Communication Received from the Government of the Netherlands.*

IMO Marine Environment Protection Committee Resolution MEPC 71/17/Add. 1 Annex 2, of 2017, *Draft Amendments to Regulation B-3 of the BWM Convention.*

IMO Marine Environment Protection Committee Resolution MEPC.127(53), of 22 July 2005, *Guidelines for Ballast Water Management and Development of Ballast Water Management Plans (G4).*

IMO Marine Environment Protection Committee Resolution MEPC.151(55), of 13 October 2006, *Guidelines on Designation of Areas for Ballast Water Exchange (G14).*

IMO Marine Environment Protection Committee Resolution MEPC.152(55), of 13 October 2006, *Guidelines for Sediment Reception Facilities (G1).*

IMO Marine Environment Protection Committee Resolution MEPC.157(55), of 13 October 2006, *Recommendation on Standards for the Rate of Discharge of Untreated Sewage from Ships.*

IMO Marine Environment Protection Committee Resolution MEPC.169(57), of 4 April 2008, *Procedure for Approval of Ballast Water Management Systems that Make Use of Active Substances (G9).*

IMO Marine Environment Protection Committee Resolution MEPC.184(59), of 17 July 2009, *Guidelines for Exhaust Gas Cleaning Systems.*

IMO Marine Environment Protection Committee Resolution MEPC.209(63), of 2 March 2012, *Guidelines on Design and Construction to Facilitate Sediment Control on Ships (G12).*

IMO Marine Environment Protection Committee Resolution MEPC.227(64), of 5 October 2012, *Guidelines on Implementation of Effluent Standards and Performance Tests for Sewage Treatment Plants.*

IMO Marine Environment Protection Committee Resolution MEPC.259(68), of 15 May 2015, *Guidelines for Exhaust Gas Cleaning Systems.*

IMO Marine Environment Protection Committee Resolution MEPC.275(69), of 22 April 2016, *Establishment of the Date on Which Regulation 11.3 of MARPOL Annex IV in Respect of the Baltic Sea Special Area Shall Take Effect.*

IMO Marine Environment Protection Committee Resolution MEPC.279(70), of 28 October 2016, *Guidelines for Approval of Ballast Water Management Systems (G8).*

IMO Marine Environment Protection Committee Resolution MEPC.287(71), of 7 July 2017, *Implementation of the BWM Convention.*

IMO Maritime Safety Committee Resolution MSC.98(73), of 5 December 2000, *The International Code for Fire Safety Systems*.

IMO Maritime Safety Committee Resolution MSC.367(93), of 22 May 2014, *Amendments to the International Code for Fire Safety Systems (FSS Code)*.

IMO, Comprehensive Information on the Status of Multilateral Conventions and Instruments in Respect of which the International Maritime Organization or its Secretary-General Performs Depositary or Other Functions, 2 March 2021, <https://www.imo.org/en/About/Conventions/Pages/StatusOfConventions.aspx> (accessed 7 March 2021).

### *Websites*

CDNI, 'Guide CDNI: Pour l'application des dispositions relatives à l'élimination des déchets et à l'utilisation de produits de nettoyage conformément à la CDNI' 2016, at: <https://www.cdni-iwt.org/wp-content/uploads/2016/01/Brochure-CDNI-nettoyage-2016-FR.pdf> (accessed 17 November 2020).

CDNI, 'Résidus de Curage et Gaz Inertes' 2020, at: <https://www.cdni-iwt.org/faq/divers/> (accessed 17 November 2020).

CDNI, 'The Convention' 2020, at: <https://www.cdni-iwt.org/presentation-of-cdni/?lang=en> (accessed 17 November 2020).

EMSA, 'Ballast Water' 2020, at: <http://emsa.europa.eu/implementation-tasks/environment/ballast-water.html> (accessed 17 November 2020).

IMO, 'Ballast Water Management' 2020, at: <https://www.imo.org/en/OurWork/Environment/Pages/BallastWaterManagement.aspx> (accessed 17 November 2020).

IMO, 'Emission Control Areas (ECAs) designated under MARPOL Annex VI' 2020, at: <https://www.imo.org/en/OurWork/Environment/Pages/Emission-Control-Areas-(ECAs)-designated-under-regulation-13-of-MARPOL-Annex-VI-(NOx-emission-control).aspx> (accessed 17 November 2020).

IMO, 'Equivalents (SOx scrubber, etc.) – Regulation 4' 2020, at: <https://www.imo.org/en/OurWork/Environment/Pages/Equivalents-(Sox-scrubber,-etc.)---Regulation-4.aspx> (accessed 17 November 2020).

IMO, 'International Convention for the Prevention of Pollution from Ships (MARPOL)' 2020, at: <https://www.imo.org/en/About/Conventions/Pages/International-Convention-for-the-Prevention-of-Pollution-from-Ships-(MARPOL).aspx> (accessed 17 November 2020).

IMO, 'List of IMO Conventions' 2020, at: <http://www.imo.org/en/About/Conventions/ListOfConventions/Pages/Default.aspx> (accessed 17 November 2020).

IMO, 'Prevention of Air Pollution from Ships' 2020, at: <https://www.imo.org/en/OurWork/Environment/Pages/Air-Pollution.aspx> (accessed 17 November 2020).

IMO, 'Prevention of Pollution by Sewage from Ships' 2020, at: <https://www.imo.org/en/OurWork/Environment/Pages/Sewage-Default.aspx> (accessed 17 November 2020).

IMO, 'Sulphur oxides (SOx) and Particulate Matter (PM) – Regulation 14' 2020, at: <https://www.imo.org/en/OurWork/Environment/Pages/Sulphur-oxides-(SOx)-%E2%80%93-Regulation-14.aspx> (accessed 17 November 2020).

IMO, 'Sulphur 2020: Cutting Sulphur Oxide Emissions' 2020, at: <https://www.imo.org/en/MediaCentre/HotTopics/Pages/Sulphur-2020.aspx> (accessed 17 November 2020).

### *Case-Law of International Courts and Tribunals*

*The "ARA Libertad" Case (Argentina v. Ghana)*, Provisional Measures, Order of 15 December 2012, *ITLOS Reports* 2012, 332.

*Chagos Marine Protected Area Arbitration (Mauritius v. United Kingdom)*, Award, 18 March 2015, PCA Case No. 2011-03.

*Dispute Concerning Coastal State Rights in the Black Sea, Sea of Azov, and Kerch Strait (Ukraine v. the Russian Federation)*, Award concerning the Preliminary Objections of the Russian Federation, 21 February 2020, PCA Case No. 2017-06.

*Request for an Advisory Opinion Submitted by the Sub-Regional Fisheries Commission (SRFC)*, Advisory Opinion, 2 April 2015, *ITLOS Reports* 2015, 4.

*South China Sea Arbitration (Republic of the Philippines v. People's Republic of China)*, Award, 12 July 2016, PCA Case No. 2013-19.

*Southern Bluefin Tuna Cases (New Zealand v. Japan; Australia v. Japan)*, Provisional Measures, Order of 27 August 1999, *ITLOS Reports* 1999, 280.

### *Case-Law of the European Court of Justice*

Judgment of the European Court of Justice (ECJ) in Case C-461/13 *Bund für Umwelt und Naturschutz v Germany*.

Judgment of the European Court of Justice (ECJ) in Case C-194/94 *CIA Security International SA v Signalson SA and Securitel SPRL*.

Judgment of the European Court of Justice (ECJ) in Case C-6/64 *Costa v E.N.E.L.*

Judgment of the European Court of Justice (ECJ) in Case C-6/03 *Deponiezweckverband Eiterköpfe v Land Rheinland-Pfalz*.

Judgment of the European Court of Justice (ECJ) in Cases C-379/08 and C-380/08 *ERG and others*.

Judgment of the European Court of Justice (ECJ) in Case C-232/97 *L. Nederhoff & Zn. v Dijkgraaf en hoogheemraden van het Hoogheemraadschap Rijnland*.

www.ingramcontent.com/pod-product-compliance
Lightning Source LLC
Chambersburg PA
CBHW031332230926
51848CB00001B/206
*9789004470323*